WHEN YOU'RE A CHRISTIAN,
the Whole World Is from Missouri

WHEN YOU'RE A CHRISTIAN, the Whole World Is from Missouri

Living the Life of Faith in a "Show Me" World

JAMES W. MOORE

Dimensions for Living
Nashville

WHEN YOU'RE A CHRISTIAN, THE WHOLE WORLD IS FROM MISSOURI:
LIVING THE LIFE OF FAITH IN A "SHOW ME" WORLD

This book is printed on acid-free paper.

Library of Congress Cataloging-in-Publication Data

Moore, James W. (James Wendell), 1938–
    When you're a Christian, the whole world is from Missouri : living the
life of faith in a "show me" world / James W. Moore.
        p.   cm.
    ISBN 0-687-00786-0 (pbk. : alk. paper)
    1. Christian life.   2. Moore, James W. (James Wendell), 1938–
I.   Title.
BV4501.2.M5816   1997
248.4—dc21   97-33163

Most Scripture quotations are from the New Revised Standard Version Bible,
Copyright 1989 by the Division of Christian Education of the National Council
of the Churches of Christ in the USA. Used by permission.

Those noted RSV are from the Revised Standard Version of the Bible, copyright
1946, 1952, 1971 by the Division of Christian Education of the National Council
of Churches of Christ in the USA. Used by permission.

That noted KJV is from the King James Version Bible.

Study guide by John D. Schroeder.

00 01 02 03 04 05 06 — 10 9 8 7 6 5

MANUFACTURED IN THE UNITED STATES OF AMERICA

For Paul

Contents

Introduction

When You're a Christian, the Whole World Is from Missouri

*R*ecently I flew to Oklahoma City to speak to a gathering of pastors. A young minister met my plane, and we drove out to the Retreat Center, about an hour's drive. As we reached our destination, I couldn't help noticing that the Retreat Center was located in a beautiful "old west" setting, called (of all things) Devil's Canyon! There's a sermon there somewhere! (Perhaps something about taking the gospel to the uttermost parts of the world.)

It was a great experience for me—being with those pastors in Devil's Canyon. Three days later, I was back at the airport in Oklahoma City, and while waiting for the plane to bring me home, I noticed something that fascinated me. There in the airport was a young man wearing a white T-shirt with these words emblazoned across the front: "When you're a Christian, the whole world is from Missouri."

"I like your T-shirt," I said to him.

"Thanks," he said with a grin. "It gets lots of responses, comments, and questions. Actually, it's a song title." Then he added, "You know, Missouri is the 'Show-Me State,' and in a sense, that's what the world is saying to us Christians: 'If you're a Christian, show me! Don't just talk the talk. Let's see you walk the walk.' Talking a good game is not enough. The world needs to see us really live our faith."

Well, the song title is right, and so is that young man. The world is saying to us as never before: "If you are a Christian—show me!" The point is clear. It's not enough to just hear it preached from our pulpits; it's not enough to just sing it in our hymns; it's not enough to just talk about it in our Sunday school classes. The Christian faith is a lifestyle! It's a way of living!

That's what the apostle Paul meant when he wrote these words: "Let your manner of life be worthy of the gospel of Jesus Christ." That is, show the world by your conduct, your behavior, your actions, your tone of voice, your commitments, your priorities, your love, your everyday life, that you are a Christian. And in the Sermon on the Mount, Jesus says, "You will know them by their fruits."

Jesus is actually talking about false prophets here, but the reverse is also true. Both false prophets and good prophets are known by the fruits they produce. That's the acid test. Not words, not outward appearance, not pious platitudes, not clever cliches, not spasmodic religious showboating. No! Ultimately, we are known by the fruits we bring forth in our daily lives.

A story is told about a businessman who announced to his office staff one day that he was going on a diet. However, the very next day, he arrived at the office with a large coffee cake in hand.

"What happened?" his colleagues asked. "We thought you were going on a diet."

"I was," the man replied, "but as I was on my way to the office this morning, I passed by a bakery and saw this incredibly scrumptious-looking coffee cake on display in the window. So I prayed, 'God, if you really want me to have that coffee cake for breakfast this morning, please find me a parking spot right in front of the bakery.' And sure enough, there it was—the eighth time around the block, there it was!" (Thanks to Brian Bauknight, Christ UMC Bethel Park, Pennsylvania, Sept. 26, 1993.)

Now, all of us can laugh at that, and some of us who have a "sweet tooth" can resonate strongly to it, but the truth is that it is simply not enough to "play at" religion like that. Christianity is full of joy, to be sure, but at the same time, it is serious business. It is commitment to God with all your heart, soul, mind, and strength. It is commitment to God with every fiber of your being.

You see, Christianity is not merely a set of intellectual ideas, not merely a collection of theological doctrines, not merely a series of philosophical arguments. It is a way of life! It is a lifestyle that works daily. It is not only a way of believing; it is also a way of behaving. Our Christian faith is not just something we celebrate in the sanctuary one day a week; it is something we live out in the world every day—something we demonstrate and share with others at home, in the office, on the street, on the tennis court, even on a date.

One of my favorite stories is the one about the secretary who one day expressed an ethical concern to her boss. The company was about to become involved in a business deal that she thought was morally questionable.

When she verbalized her discomfort, the boss, with some irritation, said to her, "Where in the world did you get that idea? From that funny little church you go to?" At first, the secretary was hurt by that comment, and for a few seconds she was speechless.

But then she came back with the perfect response: "I'm glad my funny little church shows!"

Now, let me ask you something: Does your funny little church show? Can people out there in the world tell that you are a Christian? When you're a Christian, everybody you meet is from Missouri. Are you showing them your faith? Let me bring this closer to home by raising three questions.

Can People Tell by the Way You Influence Others That You Are a Christian?

Our influence is so important, more important than I could ever express in words.

A few years ago at a university in the Midwest, some students in a psychology class were studying the power of positive reinforcement—the impact it has on a person when you give encouragement, and the debilitating effect that comes when positive reinforcement is withheld. One day the professor was called out of the room for a few moments. Now, leaving psychology students alone even for a few minutes is risky business, as the professor soon found out.

The students decided to have some fun with the professor, and at the same time, test his theories about "positive reinforcement." The professor was in the habit of pacing back and forth across the front of the classroom as he lectured. So every time the professor moved toward the radiator in the classroom, the students would give him dramatic positive reinforcement. They would say "Yes!" "All Right!" "Amen!" and applaud and smile, then nod and take notes like crazy!

With verbal expressions and body language, they affirmed and encouraged him as he walked toward the radiator. But when he moved away from the radiator, they did the opposite—they would moan, groan, yawn, stretch. They would put their pencils down and look out the window, or nod off like they were about to fall asleep, as if they were bored to tears.

Now, they never told the professor what they were doing, and he never figured it out. But by the end of the week, he was giving his entire lecture sitting on the radiator! That says a lot about the power of influence. But the question is: How is it with us right now? What influence are we having on others? On this community? This world? Is our influence on other people drawing them toward Christ, or pushing them away from him?

Norman Cousins once said something about Albert Schweitzer that impressed me: "The greatness of Schweitzer was not so much what he did for others, but what others have done because of him and the power of his example. This is the real measure of the man." In a sense, this is the real measure of all of us. It's not just what we do, but what we influence others to do.

Jesus spoke strong words about this. Pointing to a child one day, he said, "Whoever causes one of these little ones who believe in me to sin, it would be better for him if a great millstone were hung round his neck and he were thrown into the sea" (Matt. 18:6 RSV). Strong words—because the power of influence is so important. So, let me ask you: Can people tell by the way you influence others that you are a Christian?

Can People Tell
by the Way You Live Out the Truths of the Bible
That You Are a Christian?

As Christians, we are called to be "living Bibles," people who immerse ourselves so deeply in the Bible that it becomes part of us.

A few years ago, newscaster Ted Koppel was asked to give the commencement address at Duke University. He surprised his audience. He didn't talk about politics or international problems. He chose to speak on a subject that he thought those students needed to hear and think about most of all—morality! Personal morality! And when he finished, he received a standing ovation! In that speech, Ted Koppel said this:

> We have actually convinced ourselves that slogans will save us: "Shoot up if you must, but make sure you use a clean needle when you do." "Enjoy sex whenever and wherever you please, but always make sure that you do it safely." The answer is "No," a thousand times "No!" Not because it isn't cool or smart or because you might end up in jail or dying in an AIDS ward if you do—but just because it's wrong! We've spent 5,000 years as a race of human beings trying to drag ourselves out of the primeval slime by searching for truth and moral absolutes. And in its purest form, truth is not a polite tap on the shoulder, it is a howling reproach. What Moses brought down from Mount Sinai were not the Ten Suggestions. They were the Ten Commandments!

That day at Duke University, Ted Koppel was saying something we all need to hear—namely, that the hope of the world (the only hope) is that we take seriously the truths of the Bible, appropriate them to our lives, and live them daily. It's important to remember that God's laws and commandments are not given to us to put us in straitjackets, but rather to help us live life to the full. They are not here to hinder us, but to help us. Life is better when we love God and other people. Life is better when we are honest and loyal and truthful and kind and caring. God knew that—and that's why he gave us the great truths of the Bible to live by.

But the question is: How is it with you right now? Can people see the Bible in you? Can people tell by the way you influence others and by the way you live out the truths of the Bible that you are a Christian?

Can People Tell
by the Way You Support the Church
That You Are a Christian?

My friend Norman Neaves tells about a young woman in his church who was expressing her fears one day. She had just gone through a divorce and found herself anxious and fearful about the future.

"If it were just me," she said, "I'd be okay. Oh yes, I would hurt and I would feel lonely, and I would have to do without some things, but I know I could handle it just fine. It's my three kids I'm worried about." And then she added, "So many of their friends have new clothes to wear to school this year. And not just new clothes, but expensive clothes—you know, Cole-Haan's and Polo's and things like that. There's no way I can afford things like that now. And when they reach college age, what in the world will I do then? We're just barely making it as it is." With that, her voice trailed off and she began to cry.

An older woman put her arm around her and tried to comfort her. "I know just how you feel," she said. "I was in your place twenty years ago. My husband left me, I had four little kids under nine years old, and I wasn't making even $500 a month. But let me tell you something: We made it, the five of us. And I'm so proud of who and where my kids are today. I'd put them up against anybody's kids."

And listen to this. She looked at the younger woman and said, "I have only one piece of advice to give you. It's the best advice I know. Make sure that you and your children go to church and Sunday school every week. That might not seem like much to you right now, but I can't tell you what a difference it will make in the long run. They'll receive something there that many kids don't receive, and it's something they can build their lives on for the rest of their days. Church is the best gift you can give your kids! Don't ever forget that!"

So many parents don't realize that what really pays off is not what they give their children on the outside, but what they give them on the inside—how they nurture them within. The best way to give them what they need within is to give them the church, to give them Christ and his church—and let them see us supporting the church. What better thing can we do for our children than keep the church alive and well in their lives and in ours? What better thing can we do for our community? For our world? What better way can we express our love for our Lord than to be loyal to his church, to support it with our prayers, our presence, our gifts, and our service?

The saying, "When you're a Christian, the whole world is from Missouri" means: Show me your Christian faith! Show me by the way you influence others for good. Show me by the way you live out the truths of the Bible. Show me by the way you support the church that you are a Christian. Join me now as we explore some of the important Christian characteristics that others should see in us.

Chapter 1

Can the World See Your Christian Gumption?

*Y*ou have heard that it was said, 'An eye for an eye and a tooth for a tooth.' But I say to you, Do not resist an evildoer. But if anyone strikes you on the right cheek, turn the other also; and if anyone wants to sue you and take your coat, give your cloak as well; and if anyone forces you to go one mile, go also the second mile. Give to everyone who begs from you, and do not refuse anyone who wants to borrow from you."

—MATTHEW 5:38-42

In 1994, Forrest Gump took America by storm! The simple story of a good-hearted fellow from Alabama—with an I.Q. of 75—a fellow who stumbled through two decades of history, touched the hearts of millions of Americans. Soon after the movie *Forrest Gump* was released, it topped the $100 million mark. The novel has sold more than a million copies, and another book titled *Gumpisms: The Wit and Wisdom of Forrest Gump* sold over a quarter of a million copies in its first few weeks. It's simply a compilation of Forrest Gump sayings, such as "Stupid is as stupid does," or "Life is like a box of chocolates, you never know what you are going to get."

What is the appeal of *Forrest Gump?* The director of the movie, Robert Zemeckis, admitted to *Newsweek* magazine that he was surprised by the way the film hit the cultural chord of our nation. Even the novel's author, Winston Groom, can't explain the phenomenon.

"I wasn't trying to send a message when I wrote the novel," he says. "I think I was simply trying to say that here is this man of great dignity who tries to maintain his dignity when he is put into a number of undignifying situations."

Atlanta psychiatrist Frank Pittman sees the appeal of *Forrest Gump* as a strong backlash against the prevailing cynicism of our time: "This movie is a confirmation that nice guys can finish first—that following the rules is not foolish. In the movie, we're seeing our whole history through the eyes of somebody who sees goodness everywhere he looks, who believes a promise is a promise, and that if he follows the rules everything will be O.K." (*The Atlanta Journal,* Aug. 9, 1994).

Others say the popularity of the film is rooted in the outstanding performances of the actors. Still others point to the technical wizardry of the movie. The computer magic that not only put Tom Hanks in authentic historic footage, but also enabled him to interact with President Kennedy, President Johnson, President Nixon, and Governor Wallace was indeed amazing and impressive. However, I think the appeal of *Forrest Gump* goes deeper still. I believe the appeal of the movie is found—if you will pardon the pun—in Forrest Gump's "Christian Gumption."

The word *Christian* means "Christlike," and the word *gumption* means "boldness, courage, wisdom, resourcefulness, strength." Forrest Gump has a simple faith which he lives boldly. He lives life unselfishly. He loves people unconditionally. He trusts God unreservedly. That basic outline is not only a summation of Forrest Gump's life, it also is a pretty good synopsis of the teachings of Jesus in the Sermon on the Mount.

When Jesus says things such as "Be humble-minded," "Be obedient," "Be merciful," "Be pure in heart," "Be peacemakers," "Be the salt of the earth and the light of the world," "Turn the other cheek," "Go the second mile," "Love your enemies and pray for those who persecute you," "Be perfectly loving like your Father in heaven is loving," he means "Have Christian Gumption!" Be bold and confident and courageous and strong. Live boldly in the spirit of Christ, and trust God to bring it out right.

In other words, live life unselfishly! Love people unconditionally! Trust God unreservedly! These three ideas represent a summation of what scholars call the hard sayings of Jesus. Let's take a look at each of these sayings.

To Have "Christian Gumption" Means to Live Life Unselfishly

All through the Gospels, Jesus underscores the theme of sacrifice. Then he goes to the cross to show us that he meant what he said. "To live life unselfishly"—that was a key motif of Jesus' life and teachings, and it is a key characteristic of the Christian lifestyle.

Sometimes when I go in a bookstore and see all the books on topics such as the effective use of power, how to win by intimidation, how to manipulate people and get your way every time, how to negotiate from power, I often wonder what Jesus would think about these kinds of books and power politics. I think he would be turned off by the "me-ism" approach to life, because it goes so directly against the grain of everything he taught and stood for.

One of the most beautiful moments in *Forrest Gump* is that scene where Forrest has become rich—as he puts it, "a gazillionaire"—through his work in the shrimp business. And he takes half of his fortune and gives it to the mother of his friend Bubba. His African American friend Bubba didn't come home from Vietnam, so Forrest unselfishly shares his wealth with Bubba's family. There is something very Christlike about that; it takes "Christian Gumption" to live life unselfishly.

I once heard Drayton McLane, the owner of the Houston Astros and a devout Christian, speak to a group in Houston. He told about a meeting of the twenty-eight owners of the major league baseball teams that was held one winter. The widow of Jackie Robinson came in to speak to the owners. Jackie Robinson was the first African American to play baseball in the major leagues. He broke that racial barrier in 1947 when he went to play for the Brooklyn Dodgers. He played for ten major-league seasons and had a lifetime batting average of 311. He helped the Dodgers win six National League pennants and led the Dodgers to a World Series championship in 1955. He was an all-star numerous times and was voted into the Baseball Hall of Fame in 1962.

When his widow came to speak to the owners, McLane said they fully expected her to talk about Robinson's life and career on the baseball diamond. They expected her to describe how he broke the barrier to let African Americans play baseball in the major leagues and all the pressures they were under at the time. But interestingly, she didn't mention any of that. Rather, she said this: "What you accomplish in athletics is not important. What you accomplish in business is not important. All that matters is what you do for others!" She concluded with this statement: "A life is not important except for its impact on other people's lives."

Where did she learn that? You know, don't you? She learned that at church. She learned that from Jesus. She learned that from our Lord, who said, "The greatest among us is the one who serves." She learned that from the One who went unselfishly to the cross to give himself up for you and me.

But this is the question: When will we ever learn? When will we ever wake up? When will we ever take seriously the command and witness of Jesus? When will we ever have the "Christian Gumption" to live life unselfishly?

To Have "Christian Gumption" Means to Love People Unconditionally

Toward the end of Matthew, chapter 5, we find those often quoted words about God letting his rain fall on both the just and the unjust. More often than not, we quote this verse when trouble comes: "Well," we say, "problems and sorrows come to all of us." And that's O.K., because that idea is indeed helpful. But if you will look closely at the context of this passage, you will discover that what Jesus is really talking about here is love—unconditional love— the love of God falling like rain on all alike!

That's the way God loves—unconditionally! Now, we may reject his love, we may ignore his love, we may spurn his love, we may turn away from his love; but like gentle persistent rain, God's love falls on all of us. He just keeps on loving us. In the church we have a special word for this: grace. Amazing grace! God loves us not because we are good, but because he is good!

Here's the catch: God wants us to love like that! He wants us to imitate his gracious, generous, compassionate, merciful, loving ways! That's what this strange-sounding verse at the end of chapter five is all about. "You, therefore, must be perfect, as your heavenly Father is perfect" (RSV). In this context, the word "perfect" means *loving*. In Luke's Gospel, it is translated like this: "Be merciful, even as your Father is merciful" (6:36 RSV).

In the movie *Forrest Gump,* we see unconditional love in the way Forrest relates to Jenny. Jenny keeps running away, but Forrest keeps on loving her, forgiving her, defending her, seeking her, protecting her, helping her. His love for her is complete and unconditional. To love like that takes "Christian Gumption"!

In *The Grand Essentials,* Ben Patterson writes these powerful words:

> I have a theory about old age. . . . When life has whittled us down, when joints have failed and skin has wrinkled and capillaries have clogged and hardened, what is left of us will be what we were all along, in our essence.
>
> Exhibit A is a distant uncle. . . . All his life he did nothing but find new ways to get rich. . . . He spent his [days] very comfortably, drooling and babbling constantly about the money he had made. . . . When life whittled him down to his essence, all there was left was raw greed. . . . That is what he had cultivated in a thousand little ways over a lifetime.
>
> Exhibit B is my wife's grandmother. . . . When she died in her mid-eighties, she had already been senile for several years. What did this lady talk about? The best example I can think of was when we asked her to pray before dinner. She would reach out and hold the hands of those sitting beside her, a broad, beautific smile would spread across her face, her dim eyes would fill with tears as she looked up to heaven, and her chin would quaver as she poured out her love to Jesus. That was Edna in a nutshell. She loved Jesus and she loved people. She couldn't remember our names, but she couldn't keep her hands from patting us lovingly whenever we got near her.
>
> When life whittled her down to her essence all there was left was love: love for God and love for people. (Waco, Tex.: Word Books, 1942 [pp. 109-10]).

But the question is this: When will we ever learn? When will we ever wake up? When will we ever take seriously the command and witness of Jesus? When will we ever find the "Christian Gumption" to live life unselfishly and to love people unconditionally?

To Have "Christian Gumption" Means to Trust God Unreservedly

This is one of the key themes of the Sermon on the Mount, and it was a basic motif of Jesus' life: Trust God unreservedly. Do the best you can and trust God to bring it out right. Don't quit! Don't give up! Don't throw in the towel! No matter how tough life gets, keep on living the faith, and keep on trusting God to bring the victory in his own good time.

One of the most poignant scenes in *Forrest Gump* is that moment when Forrest's former commanding officer in Vietnam, Lieutenant Dan, complains about God and religion and life. Lieutenant Dan is disillusioned and bitter. He lost both legs in Vietnam, and he is angry with God and with life. So he ventilates with Forrest. Lieutenant Dan spews out his hostilities with profane and irreverent complaints. He pelts heaven with his harsh words. He screams and shakes his fist at heaven. Writer Cynthia Astle describes the scene:

> As Lieutenant Dan's tirade winds down, Forrest responds [with these simple words]: "I'm going to heaven, Lieutenant Dan." Forrest Gump's gentle certainty of salvation stills Dan's outrage and helps the crippled and disillusioned Dan make the first move toward his own redemption. . . . In that moment, Jesus' instructions that one must become like a little child to enter the Kingdom shines through Forrest Gump like sunlight through a chapel window. He trusts God unreservedly. (*United Methodist Reporter,* July 22, 1994, p. 4)

The gospel song says it well: "We know not what the future holds, but we know who holds the future." But the question is this: When will we ever learn? When will we ever wake up? When will we ever take seriously the command and witness of Jesus? When will we ever find the "Christian Gumption" to live life unselfishly, to love people unconditionally, and to trust God unreservedly?

When you're a Christian, the whole world is from Missouri, saying, "Show me your Christian Gumption."

Chapter 2

CAN THE WORLD SEE YOUR SPIRIT OF FORGIVENESS?

*T*hen Peter came and said to him, "Lord, . . . how often should I forgive? As many as seven times?" Jesus said to him, "Not seven times, but, I tell you, seventy-seven times. For this reason the kingdom of heaven may be compared to a king who wished to settle accounts with his slaves. When he began the reckoning, one who owed him ten thousand talents was brought to him; . . . the slave fell on his knees before him, saying, 'Have patience with me, and I will pay you everything.' And out of pity for him, the lord of that slave released him and forgave him the debt. But that same slave, as he went out, came upon one of his fellow slaves who owed him a hundred denarii; and seizing him by the throat, he said, 'Pay what you owe.' Then his fellow slave fell down and pleaded with him, 'Have patience with me, and I will pay you.' But he refused; then he went and threw him into prison until he would pay the debt. When his fellow slaves saw what had happened, they were greatly distressed, and they went and reported to their lord all that had taken place. Then his lord summoned him and said to him, 'You wicked slave! I forgave you all that debt because you pleaded with me. Should you not have had mercy on your fellow slave, as I had mercy on you?' "*

—MATTHEW 18:21-33

Some time ago I boarded a plane in Houston to head for a meeting in New York. When I arrived at my assigned seat, I discovered that I would be sitting next to a young mother and her six-month-old baby boy.

As I buckled in, she looked at me apologetically and said, "I'm sorry. I hope my baby won't bother you on this long flight."

"Not at all," I replied. "I'm a dad and a granddad, and I love children. I feel like the luckiest person on this plane to get to sit next to you and your baby."

She smiled, and we began to chat. She asked about my profession and when I told her that I am a minister, she beamed. She immediately began to tell me how much she loves the church, what the church has meant to her and her family, and how she and her husband are trying so hard to be good Christian parents for their children. Just then, as only a mother can, she hugged her baby and kissed him tenderly.

"What's your baby's name?" I asked.

Proudly, she told me: "Joseph." And then she said, "Let me tell you something funny about that. Joseph is six months old now, and he has an older sister named Rachel, who is five years old. When her new baby brother was about to be born, she asked me what we were going to name him, and I said, 'Well, Rachel, what would you like to name him?'

"Immediately, Rachel answered, 'Joseph! I want to name him Joseph!' And then she went on, 'Momma, if we name him Joseph, I promise I won't sell him into Egyptian slavery!' "

Isn't that amazing? Obviously, Rachel was referring to that story in the book of Genesis where the great Bible character Joseph was sold into Egyptian slavery by his jealous older brothers.

"That is funny," I said to the young mother. "But how in the world did five-year-old Rachel know that story?"

She replied, "Well, Rachel is very active, and she has a short attention span. The only way I can keep her still at the dinner table at night is to promise to read her a Bible story after the evening meal."

She paused and then continued, "I have this wonderful book of Bible stories for children, and Rachel just loves it. So every night when we sit down for dinner, we have the blessing, then the meal, and then I read one of the Bible stories. Rachel loves that one about Joseph and his coat of many colors. And she loves the one where Jesus spits on the ground, makes clay, and then uses the clay to heal the blind man. But her all-time favorite is the one where the king forgives his servant, but the servant refuses to forgive his coworker."

"Why do you think that's her favorite?" I asked.

The young mother replied, "I wondered about that too, so I asked her, and she said, 'I like that one best of all because it teaches us that God is nice, and he wants us to be nice.'"

Out of the mouths of little children! Rachel is right on target, isn't she? That is precisely what Jesus is teaching us in this great parable in Matthew 18. God is loving and wants us to be loving. God is gracious and wants us to be gracious. God is forgiving and wants us to be forgiving. God is merciful and wants us to be merciful. God is compassionate and wants us to be compassionate. Or as five-year-old Rachel might put it: God is nice to us and wants us to be nice to each other!

The Scriptures are very clear about this. When it comes to forgiveness, we, as Christians, are called to imitate the forgiving spirit of God. The Scriptures point out very dramatically that we are to forgive others as graciously, lovingly, mercifully, and thoroughly as God in Christ forgives us. Jesus sums it up in Luke 6, when he says: "Be merciful, even as your Father [in heaven] is merciful" (RSV). Here in Matthew 18, in the parable of the unmerciful servant, Jesus underscores the importance of the forgiving spirit.

Remember the parable with me. It's like a one-act play with three scenes, illustrating graphically the power and beauty of forgiveness and exposing dramatically the ugliness of the unforgiving spirit.

In Scene One, a servant is brought before the king. This servant owes the king an astounding debt, a humongous debt: ten thousand talents, or ten million dollars. Let me put that in perspective. In that time, a young slave could be bought for one talent (about a thousand dollars), and this servant owes the king 10,000 talents. That's the equivalent of 10,000 slaves. If this debt were put into coins, it would take 8,600 people to carry it, with each person carrying 60 pounds of coins, and the carriers would form a line five miles long! We are talking big money here.

At that time, the total amount of the annual taxes for the five geographical regions of Judea, Idumea, Samaria, Galilee, and Perea came to only 800 talents. And this one servant owes 10,000 talents—millions of dollars—and he can't possibly pay it back. Talk about "amazing grace." Look what happens: The man acknowledges his enormous debt and pleads for mercy. Incredibly, the king, who is a gracious man, is moved with compassion, and his heart goes out to this servant. He cancels the debt, lets him off the hook, forgives him, and sets him free.

In Scene Two, the shoe is on the other foot. The man who has just been forgiven this enormous debt of ten million dollars walks out of the palace and immediately sees a fellow servant who owes him twenty dollars. What does he do? He grabs him by the throat and says, "Pay me what you owe. Give me my twenty dollars now." The fellow servant falls to his knees and pleads for mercy. But the unmerciful servant, who only moments before received incredible forgiveness from the gracious king, has no mercy to give. There is no forgiveness in his heart, and he sends his coworker to debtors' prison.

Here we see the graphic ugliness of the unforgiving spirit. Here we see dramatically how ungrateful and mixed up we can become when we accept God's gracious forgiveness, but refuse to forgive others, refuse to live in that spirit, and refuse to pass it on to others.

In the final scene, the king is again center stage. A group of servants come to him filled with distress. They report what the unmerciful servant has done. The king is not happy. He calls in the unmerciful servant and rebukes him: "What's this I hear? I forgave your debt. Should you not have had the same kind of mercy on your fellow-servant?" Then the king casts the unmerciful servant into prison, and the curtain comes down. The play is over, but the message lingers and haunts us.

Are you at odds with anybody? Are you estranged, distanced, cut off from anybody? Has someone hurt you? Are you having a hard time forgiving that person? If so, let me make three practical and biblical suggestions about what you can do.

Recognize Your Own Need for Forgiveness

My friend Rod Wilmoth tells an interesting story about a woman in a large city who left her suburban apartment one morning for a trip downtown on the bus. She put on one of her most fashionable outfits and her favorite perfume and headed out the backdoor to catch Bus #49, which would transport her to the best shopping district in town. As she hurried out the door, she remembered to pick up a small sack of garbage that had accumulated in the kitchen, which she planned to toss in the container at the curb.

She became preoccupied, however, and forgot she had the sack of garbage in her hand, along with her other packages. So she lugged the garbage unwittingly onto the bus. Immediately, as she took her seat, she noticed a terrible stench. She became upset with the city and deter-mined then and there to write an angry letter to protest this awful odor on the city bus. She opened the window, but still the stench was there. She decided that the neighborhood through which she was riding must smell awful.

"Some people just don't know how to live," she muttered to herself. "They just aren't very clean."

When she arrived at the shopping district, she discovered a horrible stench in every single store she visited.

"The whole world smells terrible. The whole world is going to the dogs," she complained.

When she finally returned home and opened her packages, only then did she realize where the terrible odor was coming from! (Rod Wilmoth, St. Paul UMC, Sept. 12, 1993, quoting J. Angell, *Accept No Limitations*, Abingdon Press).

Maybe we would be more inclined to forgive others if we first would recognize the garbage we are carrying around in our own lives. The great African American spiritual puts it like this: "It's me, It's me, It's me, O Lord, standing in the need of prayer."

I'll never forget a conversation that took place in the football locker room when I was in the tenth grade. Some of the players were griping and complaining and bashing Eddie, one of our teammates, who had dropped a pass in the end zone. We lost the game and the players were crucifying Eddie—behind his back—with hard, angry words: "Eddie cost us the game. It's all his fault. Anybody could have caught that ball. He's terrible! If I were the coach, I would kick him off the team. He's a coward. He dropped it because he's so scared."

On and on they went, ripping Eddie apart—all except a senior named George, one of the most highly respected players on the team. He just sat there quietly, slowly unlacing his shoes. Suddenly, they noticed that George was not participating in the verbal massacre of Eddie. They tried to involve him in the cruel gossip: "Hey, George, wasn't that terrible how Eddie lost the game for us?"

I'll never forget how George handled the situation. He said, "You know, I have way too many faults of my own to be critical of anybody else. And besides, I imagine right about now that Eddie feels worse than any of us." That promptly ended the cruel bashing session; it also revealed why George was one of the most highly respected players on the team.

Whenever we have a hard time forgiving someone who has done something hurtful to us, it helps to remember that the first step is to recognize our own clay feet, our own need to be forgiven.

Accept God's Gracious Forgiveness

God's forgiveness is available to us, but he won't force it on us. We have to accept it.

Some years ago, Bishop Willis J. King, the first African American bishop in America to receive a Ph.D in Old Testament, told a true story that touched me deeply. Upon his graduation from Wiley College, he went back home to spend a few days with his parents. He showed them his degree. He was so proud of it.

Then he announced, "Tomorrow I'm going to go to the downtown bank, and I'm going to borrow $500 to buy my first automobile."

The next morning, as he was about to leave, his father said to him, "Son, don't you want me to go with you and cosign your note?"

He answered, "No, Dad, I can take care of this by myself. After all, I've got my degree now." And so he went on downtown to the bank.

The bank manager said to the young man, "So you want to borrow $500. Tell me, what do you have for collateral? If you're going to get $500 from this bank, you've got to have something of equal value."

"Oh yes, sir," young King said, "I've got my degree."

The bank officer replied, "Son, I'm sorry, but we can't use that degree as collateral for $500. I'm afraid you'll just have to go elsewhere."

Bishop King was in a state of embarrassment and failure when he heard a familiar voice. His dad said, "Son, I've come to cosign your note."

"But Dad," King said, "you can't even write. All you can do is make an 'X.'"

And the banker said, "It may be true that your dad can't write and all he can do is make an 'X'. But I want to tell you something. It's that 'X' that got the loan to get you into school. It's that 'X' that got the loan to keep you in school, and it's that 'X' that got the loan that got you out of school. And if you are going to get a loan from this bank to buy a car, it's that same 'X' that's going to get the loan for you!"

King said that as he watched his dad make his "X" on that bank document, he realized that if you turned the "X" just a bit, it made the sign of the cross.

He summed up that story like this: "In that moment, I realized something more powerfully than ever before—namely, how inadequate I am, how needy I am, how insufficient I am alone, and how on Calvary's cross, Jesus cosigned my note! I wouldn't be here tonight if he hadn't. Love lifted me, when nothing else could help. Love lifted me" ("Unlearned Lessons: Excerpts from Zan Holmes," *New World Outlook,* July/August 1993).

If we want to be able to forgive, first we must recognize our own need of forgiveness; second, we must accept God's gracious gift of forgiveness.

Pass on That Forgiveness to Others

We live daily in the spirit of forgiveness. We become the instruments of God's love and peace. We become conduits of his grace and mercy.

In *The Hiding Place,* Corrie ten Boom tells of her suffering in German concentration camps during World War II. Miraculously, she survived that horrendous experience. After the war, she traveled extensively, speaking and telling of God's grace through those horrible years. On one occasion in Munich, a man came up to her after she had finished speaking. She recognized him. He had been a prison guard in Ravensbruck, a man who had been very cruel to her and her sister, but evidently had become a Christian after the war. He did not recognize her.

He extended his hand to her and said, "How grateful I am for your message, *Fraulein*. To think that, as you say, He has washed my sins away!"

All the horrible memories of the past flooded into her mind. She struggled to raise her hand, but it remained at her side. She prayed, "Lord Jesus, forgive me and help me to forgive him." Nothing happened. Again she prayed, "Jesus, I cannot forgive him. Give me your forgiveness."

She describes what happened next: "As I took his hand, the most incredible thing happened. From my shoulder along my arm and through my hand a current seemed to pass from me to him, while into my heart sprang a love . . . that almost overwhelmed me."

Has someone been cruel to you? Has someone hurt you deeply? Maybe you think there's no way you could ever forgive that person. On your own strength, you probably can't. But you *can* ask Christ to give you his forgiveness. You can ask for his help. Let the power of his forgiveness flow through you. Let his gracious spirit be your spirit. That's how it works. We recognize our need of forgiveness, we accept God's gracious gift of forgiveness, and then we pass it on. We pass the forgiveness to others.

When you're a Christian, the whole world is from Missouri, saying, "Show me your spirit of forgiveness."

Chapter 3

CAN THE WORLD SEE YOUR DEDICATION?

*W*hen they had finished breakfast, Jesus said to Simon Peter, "Simon son of John, do you love me more than these?" He said to him, "Yes, Lord; you know that I love you." Jesus said to him, "Feed my lambs." A second time he said to him, "Simon son of John, do you love me?" He said to him, "Yes, Lord; you know that I love you." Jesus said to him, "Tend my sheep." He said to him the third time, "Simon son of John, do you love me?" Peter felt hurt because he said to him the third time, "Do you love me?" And he said to him, "Lord, you know everything; you know that I love you." Jesus said to him, "Feed my sheep. Very truly, I tell you, when you were younger, you used to fasten your own belt and to go wherever you wished. But when you grow old, you will stretch out your hands, and someone else will fasten a belt around you and take you where you do not wish to go." (He said this to indicate the kind of death by which he would glorify God.) After this he said to him, "Follow me."

—JOHN 21:15-19

In 1977, noted author Lyle Schaller tried to slip one past us. He wrote a book on the church titled *Survival Tactics in the Parish,* and he dedicated the book to "Shang." He described Shang as one who has mastered three of the most essential characteristics for survival in the parish ministry. He wrote, "Shang gets plenty of sleep every day, has a clear sense of self-identity, and has a remarkable ability to ignore trifling diversions."

When Leonard Sweet, the dean of Drew Theological School, picked up a copy of the book and saw that intriguing dedication to Shang, he wondered who Shang might be. When he did some investigating, he discovered that Shang was none other than Lyle Schaller's dog! Fascinated by this, Sweet rushed off to the library to do some research on book dedications. He found a large number of traditional and predictable dedications. Many authors dedicate their books to loved ones—Mom, parents, children, friends, coworkers, spouses, siblings, patrons, and pets. Then, too, some dedications were surprising and unusual. For example, one author dedicated his book to a mountain, another to a "Dear Old Apple Tree," another to old movies, and still another to a certain beloved armchair. Larry McMurtry dedicated one of his western novels to "Leslie, for the use of her goat," and Robert Morley dedicated his *Book of Worries* "to scrambled eggs on toast."

Sweet said he had two personal favorites. The first he found in a book by Stephen Pile: "To all those who have written terrible books on how to be a success. I dedicate this terrible book on how it's perfectly all right to be incompetent for hours on end, because I am . . . and so is everyone I know." The second, found in a book by a writer named Ronald, contained this brutally honest confession: "Dedicated to my creditors, whose increasing impatience has made this book necessary."

In his research, Sweet discovered that more and more authors are finding the gall to arrogantly dedicate their books to themselves. For example, one author wrote this: "I dedicate this book to me, wishing myself all happiness." Carlotta Monti, the girlfriend of W. C. Fields, wrote a book about the famous comedian and dedicated the book to herself with these words: "To myself, for the many years of loving service and kindness I willingly gave him" (Paraphrase of Leonard Sweet, "The Back Page," *Homiletics*).

Isn't that something? There's a sermon there somewhere. We live in a world where more and more people are arrogantly dedicating life to no higher purpose or cause than themselves. Isn't that sad? It raises a crucial question for us to consider and grapple with and answer—namely this: To whom—and to what—is your life dedicated? If your life were a book, how would the dedication page read? Who would be honored there?

Actually, that's what this colorful and remarkable passage in John 21 is all about. The Risen Lord is asking Simon Peter this question: "Simon, to whom and to what is your life dedicated?" "Who will be honored by your life?" Remember the story with me. It is one of the most beautiful resurrection appearances recorded in the Gospels.

The Risen Lord cooks breakfast for the disciples on the seashore, and then takes Simon Peter off to the side, away from the other disciples. Three times he asks him the same question: "Simon, do you love me?"

"Yes, Lord," Simon answers. "You know that I love you!"

"Then feed my sheep," the Risen Lord says to him.

The story ends exactly the way it started months before, with Christ at the seashore, saying to Simon these words: "Follow me!"

Now, what's going on here? What is this all about? Simply this: Jesus Christ is saying to Simon Peter, "If you love me, dedicate your life to me." If you love me, dedicate your life to continuing my ministry. But Jesus is not saying that just to Simon Peter. He is saying it to you and me, here and now: "If you love me, dedicate your life to continuing my ministry. Dedicate your life to feeding and tending and caring for my sheep."

It's a good question to raise and wrestle with: To whom and to what is your life dedicated? Who is honored by your life? If your life were a book, how would the dedication page read? The Risen Christ is speaking loud and clear. Can you hear him? He is saying: "If you love me, dedicate your life to serving my sheep!" Let's take a look at what that might mean for us today.

We Can Dedicate a Life of Kindness to Christ

If you want to do good for your church and your Christ, go out into the world and be kind to people in the name of Christ. Imitate the spirit of kindness and generosity that was so radiant in our Lord. Someone once said, "You can master church history. You can spout high-sounding theological words into the air. You can even quote verses of Scripture eloquently. But only when I see your kindness, only then do I really begin to see your faith."

Carl Howie tells of an incident that took place late one winter's night in a New York subway. It was especially cold, blustery, and bitter that night, and very few people were on the subway at that hour. At each station, the train would rumble in, screech to a stop, and open its doors, allowing a few people to come and go. At one station, a dismal-looking woman got on. Her clothes were ragged and dirty. She was either extremely tired or weak from illness, or hungry—or perhaps she had had too much to drink.

As the train lurched forward, she stumbled, slumped into a seat, and went fast asleep. She slept through the screeching and the swaying of the train. Her hands were nestled inside two of the most tattered gloves you've ever seen—so full of holes that you could see that her hands were cold and chapped and almost frostbitten. The people on the subway stared at this pitiful sight, this pathetic human derelict asleep on the subway, and you could almost read their minds: "Look at that worthless wretch. How tragic to see a woman like that! How do people allow themselves to get in such a mess? The city ought to do something about people like that."

Then a strange thing happened. A young Puerto Rican boy stood up to get off the train as it slowed to stop. He could have gone out the exit closest to him, but he chose to go past that sleeping woman. He paused in front of her for a few moments; then he removed his gloves, laid them in her lap, and got off the train. Later, when someone asked him why he had given her his gloves, his answer was simple but profound. He said, "Because I am a Christian!" He did it because of Christ. He dedicated his act of kindness to Christ.

When the Risen Lord said to Simon, "If you love me, tend my sheep," he meant, "If you love me, dedicate your life to loving-kindness." Let that be your tribute to our Lord. Dedicate a life of kindness to him.

We Can Dedicate a Life of Courage to Christ

Simon Peter realized that morning on the seashore that he didn't need to be afraid anymore. Christ had faced the worst this world can dish out, and he was victorious over it. He had conquered sin and evil and death. He had won, and now Simon knew that when Christ is on your side and by your side, you have nothing to fear. You know the rest of the story. Peter went on to become one of the most courageous leaders of the church this world has ever known. He was the one who, under the threat of tremendous persecution, said, "We ought to obey God rather than man." He lived a life of courage dedicated to the cause of Christ.

Someone once asked the great Christian Phillips Brooks why he was so confident and courageous and optimistic about life. He replied, "Because I am a Christian." As Christians, we can be courageous and confident because God is with us, and nothing—not even death—can separate us from him.

One of the most beloved and colorful sports personalities of our time was a man named Jim Valvano—"Jimmy V," as he was known affectionately to sports fans around the country. He died on April 16, 1993, after a year-long battle with cancer. He was 47 years old. He will be remembered as a great basketball coach. His North Carolina State team won the national championship in 1983, upsetting the great Houston Cougar team that featured Hakeem Olajuwon and Clyde Drexler.

Valvano will be remembered also as an outstanding TV analyst, an eloquent inspirational speaker, and a lovable, wise-cracking humorist. But most of all, he will be remembered for his courage—for the courageous way he faced a debilitating illness. A few weeks before he died, he was honored on national television, and to that vast viewing audience he said:

Today, I fight a different battle. You see, I have trouble walking and I have trouble standing for a long period of time. Cancer has taken away a lot of my physical abilities. Cancer is attacking and destroying my body. But what cancer cannot touch is my mind, my heart and my soul. I have faith in God and hope that things might get better for me. But even if they don't, I promise you this. I will never ever quit. And if cancer gets me, then I'll just try my best to go to heaven, and I'll try to be the best coach they've ever seen up there.

You know what Jim Valvano was saying, don't you? He was saying, "I'm not afraid. Because I am a Christian, I'm not afraid." As Christians, we can dedicate our courage to Christ.

We Can Dedicate a Life of Service to Christ

When the Risen Lord said, "Simon, if you love me, feed my sheep," he meant, "Give your life to this!"

There is a beautiful legend that comes out of the early church about a rich merchant who searched the Mediterranean world looking for the distinguished apostle Paul. The merchant finally found Timothy, who, in turn, introduced him to Paul. Paul and the merchant visited for several hours, and when the merchant came out, he was excited.

He said to Timothy, "I've never met anyone like him. He is the most amazing human being I've ever known. He is so serene and yet so powerful. He has done so much and given so much and sacrificed so much and helped so many people. Please tell me. What is his secret?"

"Don't you know?" asked Timothy. "Paul's secret is that he is totally committed to Jesus Christ. He is committed to Christ, heart and soul."

The merchant looked even more confused. "Is that all?" he asked.

With a smile, Timothy answered, "That, my friend, is everything!"

If you and I could get in a time machine, go back to the first century, visit with Simon Peter and the apostle Paul, and ask them, "Why have you given yourself in such devoted service to the church? Why have you risked so much and lived so sacrificially?" each in his own way would answer, "Because I am a Christian." That's what being Christian means: dedicating our lives—our kindness, our courage, and our service—to Christ and his church.

When you're a Christian, the whole world is from Missouri, saying, "Show me your dedication."

Chapter 4

CAN THE WORLD SEE YOUR RESILIENCE?

*A*s soon as it was morning, the chief priests held a consultation with the elders and scribes and the whole council. They bound Jesus, led him away, and handed him over to Pilate. Pilate asked him, "Are you the King of the Jews?" He answered him, "You say so." Then the chief priests accused him of many things. Pilate asked him again, "Have you no answer? See how many charges they bring against you." But Jesus made no further reply, so that Pilate was amazed.

Now at the festival he used to release a prisoner for them, anyone for whom they asked. Now a man called Barabbas was in prison with the rebels who had committed murder during the insurrection. So the crowd came and began to ask Pilate to do for them according to his custom. Then he answered them, "Do you want me to release for you the King of the Jews?" For he realized that it was out of jealousy that the chief priests had handed him over. But the chief priests stirred up the crowd to have him release Barabbas for them instead. Pilate spoke to them again, "Then what do you wish me to do with the man you call the King of the Jews?" They shouted back, "Crucify him!" Pilate asked them, "Why, what evil has he done?" But they shouted all the more, "Crucify him!" So Pilate, wishing to satisfy the crowd, released Barabbas for them; and after flogging Jesus, he handed him over to be crucified.

—MARK 15:1-15

One of Aesop's fables tells of a Mighty Oak Tree and a Humble Reed growing side by side on the edge of a river.

From time to time they spoke to each other, but they were not close friends because the Mighty Oak considered himself far superior to the Humble Reed. One day the Oak Tree, from its great height, said to the Reed, "Look at you! You have no pride. You bend and bow to the lightest breeze. You should be more dignified and proud, like I am. You should stand erect, as I do. No wind can make me stoop or lower myself. But look at you! How weak you are!"

Just about then a fierce storm sprang up. Lightning flashed and strong winds blew hard and shook the trees. The unbending Oak stood firm for a short while. But his very stiffness became his undoing. The storm struck hard against the Oak, tore his branches, broke his biggest boughs, and toppled him into the river.

Meanwhile, the Reed swayed and bent, letting the wind blow over him, but he did not break. And when the storm passed, he sprang back and was still growing on the edge of the river.

In a graphic way, this ancient fable portrays for us one of the most valuable and helpful of all Christian qualities: resilience—the strength to bend without breaking! We see the saga of the mighty, haughty oak versus the humble, resilient reed underscored powerfully in the trial and crucifixion of Jesus.

On the one hand, there is Pontius Pilate, the Mighty Oak; there is Herod, the Mighty Oak; there is Caiaphas, the Mighty Oak; the priests, the Sanhedrin, the Power of Rome—like mighty oaks they stand tall and proud and arrogant. But their own unbending brittleness is their downfall. On the other hand, there is Jesus. Like the Humble Reed, he bends, but he does not break!

Resilience. What does it really mean? Well, it's a big word for an even bigger spirit. The dictionary defines resilience as the ability to spring back; the strength to bounce back, to return to the original form or position after being bent or compressed. It means buoyancy, the ability to recover quickly from illness, depression, or adversity. It is not weakness, but the strength and power to withstand shock without permanent damage.

To clarify this further, let me tell you what resilience is not. It is not brittleness. It's the opposite of brittleness and self-pity. It's the opposite of haughtiness and closed-mindedness. It's the opposite of stiffness and inflexibility. It's the opposite of resentment and bitterness. Resilience means openness—the strength to bend without breaking.

In recent years, psychologists have come to understand what Jesus taught us in word and deed a long time ago—that as we face the storms of life, we need a resiliency of spirit that will bend, as a reed bends with the wind, but that will not break; the strength to take the hard knocks of life and then bounce back.

Dale Carnegie once pointed out that the manufacturers of automobile tires tried at first to make a tire that would resist the shocks of the road. It was a tire that was soon cut to pieces and torn to shreds. Then they started making tires that would give a little and absorb the shocks. Those tires are still with us. They are enduring because they are resilient. They give a little, they absorb, and then they bounce back.

As Christians, we need to learn how to take the storms of life with resilience, rather than with resentment or bitterness or self-pity. The storms do come, the winds do blow, the rains do fall; and the quality of Christian resilience can serve us well in these stressful days. As the Apostle Paul put it, "I am ready for anything, for Christ is my strength." Faith in Christ enables us to weather the storms.

They betrayed him, denied him, mocked him, cursed him, beat him, spat upon him, nailed him to a cross, but they could not break him. That Humble Reed bounced back. Likewise, through faith in Christ, that resilient spirit can be ours. Let me show you what I mean.

We Can Be Resilient in Our Disappointments and Heartaches

Disappointment is a fact of living. The storm of heartache comes to all of us. As J. Wallace Hamilton once said, "Every person's life is a diary in which he or she means to write one story and is forced to write yet another."

Milton went blind; Beethoven lost his hearing; Pasteur became a paralytic; Helen Keller was deaf, blind, and unable to speak. The apostle Paul wanted to take the church to Spain, but instead went to a prison cell in Rome; and Jesus went to a cross. But were they defeated by these disappointments? Absolutely not! They all bounced back and turned their disappointments into victories. With the help of God, each of us can do that too. Indeed, this is the spirit of the Christian; it's the spirit of resilience.

Let me tell you about a friend of mine named Madeline. Now in her seventies, she is an inspiration to everyone who knows her. She is bright, strong, cheerful, winsome, productive, and charming. Her great Christian spirit is radiant, and it has enabled her to overcome a terrific storm that has lashed at her since she was a small child. Talk about disappointment and heartache—for more than seventy years, she has battled this horrible storm called polio. Listen to her words:

> When I was three years old, I was one of the first nine people to have the disease diagnosed as polio in New York state; and I was nearly sixteen before a series of long hospital stays and endless operations enabled me to put my feet on the floor and, with the aid of heavy braces and crutches, begin to walk. I've never been able to walk across an open field, or play a game of tennis, or go to a dance. I

know the meaning of frustration. I've had to work hard on my attitudes. I couldn't permit myself to be eaten up by the virus of self-pity or jealousy toward those who possessed something without any effort, something that I have worked my head off to gain and know now that I will never have.

I have lived in a prison cell all my life, in a body that I could not control. So what am I to do? Well, the Christian answer is to move forward. If life gives us a LEMON, then we must make it into a refreshing LEMONADE.

That's exactly what Madeline has done, with the help of God and her great Christian spirit of resilience. Through faith in Christ, we too can do that. We can be resilient in our disappointments and heartaches.

We Can Be Resilient in Our Service to God

Our calling is to serve God with all we have, wherever we may be. We can't always choose our place of serving, so we need to learn how to be resilient and serve God and his church and his people where we are.

We can't all be chairman of the board, or president of the class. We can't all be soloists. We can't all be governors or poets. There are no ideal situations anyway, so we need to forget that, bounce back, and love God wherever we are.

I once read *The Shoes of the Fisherman* by Morris West. There is a powerful scene in that book in which the Russians were holding an archbishop of the Catholic Church as a political prisoner in a work camp. Conditions there were harsh, cold, deplorable, dehumanizing. The archbishop had been imprisoned for a long time when finally word came that he was to be released. He accepted the news of his freedom very calmly; he didn't jump up and down or do cartwheels.

It was baffling to those around him. "Aren't you excited? Don't you want to be free?" they said.

He answered, "I have been free a long, long time!" He went on to explain that in the early years of his imprisonment he had been bitter, resentful, and despondent; he had brooded and felt sorry for himself. But gradually he had discovered that you can serve God anywhere, if you set your mind to it, even in a hostile, frozen prison camp.

So he had ministered to the prisoners there, giving love and care and concern in a place where it was sorely needed. And little by little, the spirit of resilience enabled him to bounce back. He found the freedom to serve God and the people there—even in that awful place of slavery.

We have all heard it said many times: The key to real life is not in what happens to us outwardly; it's within that the real battles are fought and won or lost. Everything depends on the spirit with which we face things. We can't always choose the climate or circumstances, but we can choose the spirit with which we face them; and we can know that God is with us and will see us through.

That is resilience in our service to God—the strength to absorb the shocks of life and spring back, the power to bend without breaking.

We Can Be Resilient in Our Relations with Other People

When I say that we need to be resilient with others, I am not talking about weakness. I don't mean that we should be meek, mamby-pamby doormats for people to stomp on. Of course, we must not let people manipulate us or coerce us or abuse us. Certainly not. Of course, we must not chase every wind that blows or run after every fad that comes along. Of course, we must stand tall and firm for our Christian beliefs. Steadfastly, we must hold our standards high and be unflinching and unwavering in our commitments. That kind of unshakable faith is good.

But that kind of firm faith is not what I am talking about when I say we must be resilient with others. What I'm talking about is the opposite of that. I'm talking about that calloused, unbending, arrogant mind-set that is harsh, inflexible, and sometimes even cruel—the kind of narrow closed-mindedness demonstrated by those first-century church leaders who would not listen to Jesus, who would not accept Jesus, and who, because of their rigid, unbending ways, tried to kill him.

When I say, "Be resilient in your relationships with others," I simply mean, "Be gracious and kind and forgiving." In our homes, at church, with our friends and coworkers, in our neighborhoods, and even with the folks we routinely encounter in the day-to-day world, we need to be resilient and gracious and forgiving—not haughty and arrogant and inflexible. We need to live daily in the strong but gracious spirit of Christ.

Throughout his life and ministry, Jesus taught love and grace. Throughout his arrest on trumped-up charges, his unfair trial and his brutal crucifixion, he remained in that spirit, the spirit of graciousness and forgiveness. Jesus was the epitome of the resilient stance, and he wants us to live that way, too.

In his book *Love Is Eternal*, Irving R. Stone records a poignant conversation between Abraham Lincoln's wife, Mary Todd Lincoln, and a man named Parker. Parker was the secret-service agent who was supposed to guard President Lincoln the night he was shot:

> Parker entered, a heavy-faced man with half-closed lids. He trembled.
>
> "Why were you not at the door to keep the assassin out?" she asked fiercely.
>
> Parker hung his head. "I have bitterly repented it. But I just did not believe that anyone would try to kill so good a

man in such a public place. The belief made me careless.
I was attracted by the play and did not see the assassin
enter the box."

"You should have seen him. You had no business to be
careless." She fell back on the pillow, covered her face with
her hands. And then she said, "Go now, Mr. Parker. It's not
you I can't forgive. It's the assassin. I can never forgive
him!"

Then young Tad Lincoln, the son of the President, spoke:
"If Pa had lived, he would have forgiven the man who shot
him. Pa always forgave everybody."

Maybe Tad Lincoln put his finger on the very reason
America has taken Abe Lincoln to its heart. He was like
the one who said, "Father, forgive them, for they know not
what they do." In fact, Lincoln learned it from him.

Resilience, the strength to bend without breaking, the
power to absorb the shocks and then bounce back—it's a
godlike quality.

When you're a Christian, the whole world is from
Missouri, saying, "Show me your resilience."

Chapter 5

CAN THE WORLD SEE YOUR GRATITUDE?

*B*ut we appeal to you, brothers and sisters, to respect those
who labor among you, and have charge of you in the Lord and
admonish you; esteem them very highly in love because of their
work. Be at peace among yourselves. And we urge you, beloved to
admonish the idlers, encourage the fainthearted, help the weak, be
patient with all of them. See that none of you repays evil for evil,
but always seek to do good to one another and to all. Rejoice
always, pray without ceasing, give thanks in all circumstances;
for this is the will of God in Christ Jesus for you. Do not quench
the Spirit. Do not despise the words of prophets, but test everything; hold fast to what is good; abstain from every form of evil.
—1 THESSALONIANS 5:12-22

There is a story about a man who one day entered a
monastery noted for its commitment to silence. Every
person in the monastery took a disciplined vow of total
silence. They promised to not ever speak in their journey
of obedience. There was, however, one exception. At the
end of each year, they were allowed to speak two words to
the Abbot, the leader of the monastery.

A new monk arrived and immediately dedicated himself to the vow of silence. He didn't speak a single word
for one whole year. At the end of that first year, they
brought him into the Abbot's office to speak his two words.

The two words he chose to speak were, "Food bad!" He then got up from his chair and left. At the end of the second year, he returned to speak two more words to the Abbot. This time he said, "Room small!" At the end of the third year of silence, he came back to the Abbot again, and this time he said, "Bed uncomfortable!" At last, after four years of silence, he said to the Abbot, "Want out!"

"I'm not surprised," said the Abbot. "All you've done since you've been here is complain!"

Many of us can resonate with that story. The truth is that the world in which we now live is indeed full of complaints. Watch the evening news any night of the week, and it is obvious. Everywhere we look, people are complaining, and to be honest, some of it is understandable. There are troubles in the job market, troubles among the nations, troubles in our homes, troubles in our schools, troubles on our streets. There are drug problems, crime problems, gang problems, economic problems, homeless problems, and political problems. Labor is complaining about management, and management is complaining about labor. The Democrats are complaining about the Republicans, and the Republicans are complaining about the Democrats. And everybody is complaining about the stressful, busy, harried, hectic pace of life these days. Someone has called it "Trivial Pursuit." We spend our days and nights chasing frantically after what the world calls "success." Somehow we have conceived the notion that there is only so much of the success pie left, and we'd better get ours while the getting is good. So everybody is in a frantic rush.

A few years ago, renowned author Henri Nouwen wrote a book titled *Letters to Marc About Jesus.* The book is a collection of letters to his nephew, Marc, who is a young adult and a typical "yuppie." In it, Henri Nouwen says this:

> Increasing prosperity has not made people more friendly toward one another. They're better off; but that new-found

wealth has not resulted in a new sense of community. I get the impression that people are more preoccupied with themselves and have less time than when they didn't possess so much. . . . There's less opportunity to relax, to get together informally, and enjoy the little things in life. Success has isolated a lot of people and made them lonely. . . . And the higher up you get on the ladder of prosperity, the harder it becomes to be together, to sing together, to pray together, and to celebrate life together in the spirit of thanksgiving.

The point is that we are living in a stressful, competitive, pressure-packed world, where many people get so caught up in the "rat race" that they can't seem to find time to "stop and smell the roses." Consequently, complaints and protests, gripes and grumbles, criticisms and laments, are running high these days.

But the apostle Paul grabs us by the scruff of the neck, stops us in our tracks, and gives us one of the most amazing verses in the whole Bible: "Give thanks in all circumstances; for this is the will of God in Christ Jesus for you."

The key here is to underscore the preposition *in*. Notice, Paul does not say, "Give thanks *for* all circumstances." No! He says, "Give thanks *in* all circumstances." There's a big difference between those two words. Obviously, we don't give thanks *for* cancer or heart attacks or unemployment or tragedy or costly and painful accidents, or violence or war; but *in* all those things—in everything—we can give thanks.

You know why, don't you? Because God is with us! God is always with us, in every circumstance. And if we will open our hearts to him and hold on to him in faith and hope and love, God will see us through. God will sustain us, deliver us, save us. Someone expressed it beautifully: "Rich is not what we have; it is who we have beside us." It is not material things, as nice as those are, but God's presence with us and his watchful care over us that are the real source of thanksgiving.

On another occasion, Paul put it like this: "I am ready for anything for Christ is my strength." In other words, "Bring it on! I'm ready, because Christ is beside me!"

In all things we can be grateful, because nothing, not even death, can separate us from the love of God in Christ Jesus our Lord.

Rich is not what we have; it is who we have beside us! When we have God beside us and within us, we can indeed give thanks in everything. When we have God beside us and within us, gratitude becomes the theme, the motif, the watchword, the overriding spirit of our lives. Let me underscore three ways in which gratitude should be a part of our life as Christians.

Gratitude Is the "Language" of the Christian

I once saw a cartoon that showed a tough-looking dog running angrily toward a small cat. When the little cat saw this huge dog approaching, obviously looking for a fight, the cat began to bark—not meow—and snarl ferociously. The cat's barking so startled and frightened the dog that it tucked its tail between its legs, ran away, and hid beneath a nearby house.

Then the cat turned and said, "Sometimes it helps to know a second language!" That's true, I'm sure, and I'm equally sure that the first language of the Christian is the language of gratitude.

There is a Hassidic story about a tailor who comes to his rabbi and says, "I have a problem with my prayers. If someone comes to me and says, 'Mendel, you're a wonderful tailor,' that makes me feel good. I feel appreciated. I can go on feeling good for a whole week, even longer, on the strength of one compliment like that. But if people came to me every day, one after another, hour after hour, and kept saying to me, 'Mendel, you're a wonderful tailor,' over and over again, it would drive me crazy. It would soon get to the point where I wouldn't want to listen to them anymore. I would tell them to go away and let me do my work in peace. This is what bothers me about prayer. It seems to me that if we told God how wonderful He is once a week, even once every few weeks, and just one or two of us at a time, that's all He would need. Is God so insecure that He needs us praising him every day? Three times a day, morning, noon, and night? Hundreds of people praising him? It seems to me it would drive him crazy."

The rabbi smiled and said, "Mendel, you're absolutely right. You have no idea how hard it is for God to listen to all of our praises, hour after hour, day after day. But God knows how important it is for us to utter that praise, so in His great love for us, He tolerates all of our prayers." (Harold Kushner, *Who Needs God?* p. 153)

God does not *need* our flattery, but *we* need to be thankful people and express our gratitude continually. How can we see a manger scene and not feel a surge of gratitude? How can we look at a cross and not be grateful? How can we remember what Christ did for us at Calvary and not be filled to overflowing with the spirit of thanksgiving? How can we draw a breath, lift a hand, take a step, speak a word, enjoy a meal, experience a sunrise, kneel at an altar, walk into a church, or hold a baby, and not feel gratitude? Gratitude is the stuff of which we Christians are made. An ungrateful Christian is no Christian at all!

I once read about a man who does an interesting thing as a spiritual discipline. As he pays his bills, he writes, "Thank you" in the lower left-hand corner of every check. When he pays his electric bill, he expresses his gratitude for electricity. When he pays his telephone bill, he expresses his gratitude for the miracle of communication. When he pays his mortgage, he expresses gratitude that he has a roof over his head and a comfortable place to live.

When he pays his income tax—though he says he knows the IRS computer won't notice the words—he expresses his gratitude for the privilege of freedom in this great land.

That man's constant expression of gratitude reminds us that we cannot be truly grateful for the blessings that come our way without being grateful to God. Every sincere "Thank you" is an implied "Thank you, God!"

Let me ask you to try something. Think back over your life and remember the great Christians you have known, the ones who have touched you and moved you and influenced you for good. My guess is that all of them possessed the same great quality—not arrogance, puffed-up pride, or boastfulness, but a deep spirit of thanksgiving and an ability to express the language of gratitude. Gratitude is the language of the Christian.

Gratitude Is the Fragrance of the Christian

Back in the early days of the church, a rather strong-smelling incense was burned in the worship services, and the aroma of that incense would saturate the clothing of all those present. When the people left the church, they literally smelled of incense. Wherever they went, people could tell by their fragrance that they had been to church, that they had been in the presence of God. Today, the fragrance of the Christian is gratitude—unconditional gratitude in all circumstances. Can people sense the aroma of thanksgiving in you?

Isn't it fascinating to note that so many of the greatest expressions of thanksgiving in history came from people who did not have a lot of material blessings to count: Jesus, who had no place to lay his head; Luther, in hiding for his life; Francis of Assisi, who was voluntarily poor; the Pilgrims, cold, hungry, and scared at Plymouth Rock;

Helen Keller, blind and deaf; Mother Teresa, who lives her days in a leper colony.

Unconditional gratitude—gratitude with no strings attached—was the fragrance of their lives, because they knew God was with them. Life was hard and times were tough, but God was with them, and that's all that mattered. Gratitude is the fragrance of the Christian.

Gratitude Is the Lifestyle of the Christian

Noted minister Roland Perdue keeps an old rope in the trunk of his car. But he also cut off a part of that rope and keeps it—of all things—in his pulpit. It's a dramatic reminder of something that happened years ago when his car slid off a slick road and landed in a ditch. A farmer came by, tied a rope to the car, and pulled it out.

"How can I ever thank you?" Perdue asked him.

"Well," said the farmer, "there are lots of ways to say thanks, and the best way is to pass it on." Then he tossed the rope to Perdue and said, "Why don't you take this rope, and maybe someday you can help somebody. Maybe someday you can pull somebody out of a ditch."

Many years ago, Jesus Christ tossed us a rope, a lifeline—or better put, a cross—to remind us that Thanks-giving is thanks-living. I carry a small cross in my pocket. With it came a poem by Verna Thomas that says it all:

> I carry a cross in my pocket, a simple reminder to me
> Of the fact that I am a Christian, no matter where I may
> be.

Gratitude—that's what it's all about. It's the language of the Christian. It's the fragrance of the Christian. It's the lifestyle of the Christian.

When you're a Christian, the whole world is from Missouri, saying, "Show me your gratitude."

Chapter 6

CAN THE WORLD SEE YOUR FAITH?

*B*ut *Mary stood weeping outside the tomb. As she wept, she bent over to look into the tomb; and she saw two angels in white, sitting where the body of Jesus had been lying, one at the head and the other at the feet. They said to her, "Woman, why are you weeping?" She said to them, "They have taken away my Lord, and I do not know where they have laid him." When she had said this, she turned around and saw Jesus standing there, but she did not know that it was Jesus. Jesus said to her, "Woman, why are you weeping? Whom are you looking for?" Supposing him to be the gardener, she said to him, "Sir, if you have carried him away, tell me where you have laid him, and I will take him away." Jesus said to her, "Mary!" She turned and said to him in Hebrew, "Rabbouni!" (which means Teacher). Jesus said to her, "Do not hold on to me, because I have not yet ascended to the Father. But go to my brothers and say to them, 'I am ascending to my Father and your Father, to my God and your God.' " Mary Magdalene went and announced to the disciples, "I have seen the Lord"; and she told them that he had said these things to her.*

—JOHN 20:11-18

Let me share three brief stories. See if you can find the common thread that links them together.

The first story is about a young boy who lost his contact lens while playing basketball in his own driveway. Immediately the game stopped, and everyone started looking for it. But no luck. They couldn't find the contact lens. Just then the boy's mother drove up.

"Mom," said the boy, "I lost my contact lens. We've looked and looked, but we can't find it anywhere."

The mother got down on her hands and knees, crawled around the driveway, and in less than a minute, she announced, "Here it is!"

The boys were amazed. "How did you do that?" they asked. "We looked and couldn't find it."

"Simple," she said. "You were looking for a small piece of plastic. I was looking for $150!"

The second story is about a bachelor college professor who met his bachelor colleagues for coffee one morning.

"I have some good news and some bad news," he said to them. "First, the good news: A recent student survey shows that college coeds today find middle-aged men extremely attractive. The bad news is: They think middle age is twenty-five!"

The third story revolves around something that happened to our family one Saturday morning. We went out to breakfast, but when we arrived at the restaurant, the parking lot was jam-packed. I had to back out and go down the street to find a parking place. Actually, we were only about 75 yards from the restaurant, but since we didn't get in the parking lot, it seemed far away.

I was moaning and apologizing that we would have to walk so far, when someone in the group said, "You know, if we went to a ball game at the Astrodome and got to park this close, we would feel lucky!" Indeed so.

Of course, the common thread in these three stories is the matter of perspective—the manner in which we look at things! One person looks at a glass of water and sees it half empty. Another looks and sees it half full. It's a matter of perspective. One person looks at a cross and sees a symbol of darkness and death. Another sees a symbol of life and victory. It's a matter of perspective.

That's what the Christian faith does for us: It gives us a new perspective, a new way to look at things, a new view of life and death, and a new understanding of the cross. When Mary Magdalene saw her Lord nailed to the cross on Good Friday, the cross looked evil and horrible and devastating. It was the symbol of death. But on Easter Sunday morning, she got a new perspective. Christ had come off the cross and out of the tomb, and as she looked at the cross with Easter eyes, she saw it as the symbol of life and love and amazing grace.

One of the most popular stories that came out of the Second World War was about some Marines who were shipwrecked in the South Pacific. After days of floating in a life raft, finally they saw land.

"Land ahoy!" someone shouted. They were overjoyed! Their fears began to be dispelled, and they made their way to the shore. They kissed the ground and said prayers of gratitude to God for saving them. But then very quickly, they saw signs of life on the island, and they realized they were not alone there. The island was inhabited—but by whom?

Immediately, they began to wonder: Are we safe here? We are weak and hungry, and have no weapons of defense. Will the people of this island welcome us warmly? Or will they kill us on sight? Their fears returned. Then one of the young Marines climbed a tall palm tree to see if he could scope out the island and get some indication of what they might expect from the islanders. Were they saved? Or were they doomed?

Suddenly, from the top of the palm tree, the young Marine called down to the others, "It's OK, fellas! It's OK! We're saved! I see a steeple with a cross on it! It's all right. We're saved! I see a steeple with a cross on it."

Isn't that a powerful and wonderful true story? The sign of the cross meant salvation to those Marines. It meant life! And that's what it means for us, too. We must never lose sight of the cross!

In his book *Jesus Christ and His Cross,* F. W. Dillistone wrote:

> The cross stands at the center of the Christian religion. . . . Other systems revolve around other symbols—the crescent, the sickle, the lotus flower, the spinning wheel, the sun's disk, the living flame—but Christianity revolves around a cross. . . . There is no denying the fact that when Christianity has lost touch with the cross it has grown weak, when it has renewed its contact it has renewed its strength.

Do you know why? Because the cross is the message of God, the truth of God, the victory of God, the gospel of God, acted out in human history. This is what the apostle Paul is talking about in 1 Corinthians. The word of the cross is folly to those who are perishing, but to us who are being saved, it is the power of God.

Some years ago, someone asked Pavlova, the great Russian dancer, what she meant—what she was saying—in a certain dance. She replied, "If it could be said in words, there would be no need to dance it!"

Certain truths are too big for words. They have to be dramatized, acted out. And that's why the cross and Resurrection are so important to us. There on the old rugged cross of Good Friday, and there at the empty tomb of Easter morning, God dramatized his message. God acted it out for us. And now this symbol, the sign of the cross, serves as a constant and powerful reminder for us of God's truth, God's will for us, and God's love for us. Let me put it in a simple outline that we can easily remember. The cross is the symbol of faith, hope, and love. That's the way the apostle Paul sums it up, isn't it? Faith, hope, and love! I don't know how to improve on that, so let's take a look at these.

The Cross Is the Symbol of Faith

What in the world does that mean? Well, basically, faith means that we can trust God! In the end, in his own good time, God will win, and if we want to come out winners, we had better get on God's team. God is still God, and God is still in charge of this world. The final victory will be his. The cross reminds us of that.

Now, let's be honest. Sometimes it does seem that sin and evil are on top. Sometimes it seems as if they are overwhelming us. Sometimes it seems that they have all the steam and the loudest arguments. But listen! God will win, and we can count on that. God wants to share the victory with you and me.

The cross is a constant reminder of God's victory over sin and evil and wickedness. In Gounod's opera *Faust*, there is a dramatic scene in which the Satan character is in a sword fight with the young man, Valentine. In the course of the fight, Satan breaks the sword of Valentine and is about to kill him. But at the last second, young Valentine turns his broken sword upside down, in the likeness of a cross, and the Satan character stands there paralyzed! Against the sign of the cross, the evil one is powerless! The cross is the symbol of faith because it reminds us of God's incredible victory over sin and evil. That victory is precisely what gives us the poise, the serenity, the confidence, and the blessed assurance that we love to sing about.

One of the most moving scenes in English literature comes at the close of Charles Dickens' *Tale of Two Cities*. The carts were rumbling through the crowded streets of Paris, heading toward the guillotine, where, in the most ruthless, cruel way, people's heads would be chopped off, in full view of the curious public. Heading to be executed in one cart were two prisoners: a brave man who had lost his life but found it again, and was now laying it down for a friend; beside him was a young girl. They were riding toward their death, holding hands.

Earlier in the prison, she had noticed the strength and calmness of his face and had said to him, "If I may ride with you, will you let me hold your hand? It will give me courage." So on that day as they rode together toward their place of execution, there was no fear in her eyes as she held tightly to his hand. As they reached the guillotine, she calmly looked up into the strong face of the man beside her and said, "I think you were sent to me by heaven."

That is the good news of our faith. That is the message of the cross, the promise of Easter! One has been sent to us by heaven, and come what may, he will give us strength and see us through. We can count on that. The cross is the sign of faith, the reminder that no matter what happens to us in this life, we can trust God.

The Cross Is the Symbol of Hope

If you have a pain today so great that you feel it will never go away; if you have a depression that is so heavy you feel it can never be lifted; if there is a situation in your life in which you see no possible solution, then now is especially the time for you to remember the cross and what Easter teaches us—that all trouble is temporary!

Painful Good Fridays come for all of us, but in time, they give way to the new life of Easter morning. Sometimes in this world, we are knocked down, but the cross reminds us that we can rise again, we can have a new beginning, a new start, a new life.

Some time ago, I went to a home where a great tragedy had struck. This family has endured a lot of suffering over the years, and once again calamity had struck them. The father of that family hugged me and cried like a baby. Then he grew silent, and finally he said, "Jim, I just don't know if I can stand this. I made it through the other things, but I don't see how I can make it through this one."

I was so glad that I could tell him that the Christian faith says, Oh yes, you will! Yes, you will! God will bring you through this valley to the mountaintop on the other side. He's done it before and will do it again, because nothing can separate us from God and his love. The cross reminds us that nothing, not even death, can defeat God. That is our faith, and that is our hope. The cross reminds us of this.

The Cross Is the Symbol of Love

Some years ago, a ten-year-old boy named Johnny was sitting alone on a park bench one afternoon. It was a beautiful spring day, and Johnny was watching some other kids play baseball. An older man happened by, saw Johnny sitting there, and sat down beside him. They entered into conversation. They talked about the gorgeous weather, sports, their families. Finally, the older man said, "Johnny, I want to ask you a question. If you had three wishes, what would you wish for?"

Johnny thought for a moment and then said, "First, I would wish for peace and happiness in the world. Second, I would wish everybody would join the church. And third, I would wish that my best friend Billy, who is blind, would be able to see. That's what I would wish for."

The older man seemed amazed by little Johnny's answer and, with a look of perplexity, he said good-bye and walked away. Johnny didn't understand why the man was confused by his answer. He sat there for a moment, and then he picked up his crutches and hobbled home!

Now, you know where Johnny got that gracious, loving spirit, don't you? He got it from Jesus. He got it from the one who went to the cross for you and me. He got it from the one who came out of the tomb, showing us that love is the most powerful thing in the world. On the cross, God showed us how much he loves us and how much he wants us to love one another.

Faith, hope, love—that's what the cross is about. And may Jesus keep us near the cross.

When you're a Christian, the whole world is from Missouri, saying, "Show me your faith."

Chapter 7

Can the World See Your Christian Witness?

*N*ow *when they heard this, they were cut to the heart and said to Peter and to the other apostles, "Brothers, what should we do?" Peter said to them, "Repent, and be baptized every one of you in the name of Jesus Christ so that your sins may be forgiven; and you will receive the gift of the Holy Spirit. For the promise is for you, for your children, and for all who are far away, everyone whom the Lord our God calls to him." And he testified with many other arguments and exhorted them, saying, "Save yourselves from this corrupt generation." So those who welcomed his message were baptized, and that day about three thousand persons were added. They devoted themselves to the apostles' teaching and fellowship, to the breaking of bread and the prayers.*

—ACTS 2:37-42

There is a story told about a man who was accused of some wrongdoing and was brought before a judge.

When the judge asked if he had an attorney to represent him, the man answered, "No, I can't afford one."

The judge replied, "Well, don't worry about that. I'll appoint a lawyer to represent you, and I will choose a real good one."

"I appreciate that, Judge," answered the man. "But if you really want to appoint somebody to help me, what I need most is not a real good lawyer, but several real good witnesses!"

And that's what God wants too, isn't it? Some good witnesses! Will you step forward and volunteer for that job? That's our calling as Christians—to be God's witnesses. Let's define the term. A good witness is one who knows something firsthand, one who has seen or heard or experienced something. A good witness is one who can bring the truth to light.

That is precisely what Simon Peter was doing at Pentecost. He was boldly bearing witness to the truth of God, and he was well prepared to do that. He had been one of the followers of Jesus. He had traveled with him daily. He had heard him preach and teach. With his own eyes, he had watched him perform miracles of healing. He had seen him change people's lives dramatically. Then he had witnessed the crucifixion and the resurrection. He had talked with the Risen Lord—even had breakfast with him. And he was there when Christ ascended into heaven.

In Acts 2, we read that on the day of Pentecost, Simon Peter was empowered by the Holy Spirit and stood up to speak out for Christ. So powerful was his witness that on that very day, 3,000 people were converted to Christ. He recommended his Christian faith so convincingly that on that day, 3,000 persons were baptized and brought into the church.

Obviously, we can't all be as effective as Simon Peter in our Christian witness, but through faith and commitment to God, all of us can be empowered by the Holy Spirit to recommend our religion to others meaningfully and productively. As we study closely the witness of Simon Peter at Pentecost, four things stand out:

- The power of well-spoken words.
- The power of love and inclusiveness.
- The power of real commitment to the church.
- The power that comes when we trust God.

To bring this closer to home, let me restate those four ideas in the form of personal questions. I hope you will grapple with them honestly and earnestly in your heart.

Can You Recommend Your Faith in Christ by the Way You Speak?

Peter was a powerful, effective, convincing witness that day by the way he *spoke*. Words are so important. A word can excite or depress. A word can make us glad or sad or mad. Words can inspire and lift our spirits or defeat and deflate our souls. Words can motivate and encourage, or they can crush and kill. Words can convince us to stand tall for what is right, or they can destroy hope and blast reputations. Words can offer a beautiful prayer and preach a powerful sermon, or they can incite a riot or tell a dirty joke.

The words we choose—and the way we use them—communicate more about us and our faith than we can possibly imagine. Profane words, bigoted words, hateful words, cruel words do not promote the cause of Christ or represent the spirit of Christ. They never have and never will. We dupe ourselves by calling our dirty talk mature, adult, realistic. Come on, now! What could be more immature, childish, and unrealistic? If you want to be a good witness for Jesus Christ today, clean up your act and clean up your speech. Speak the words of faith, hope, and love in a tone of compassion, kindness, and respect.

Some years ago, when I was a senior in high school and had just decided to go into the ministry, I was sitting one day in the school cafeteria. One of my classmates sat down beside me and said, "Hey, is it true what I heard, that you are going to be a minister?"

When I answered "yes," he said, "You know, Jim, I've never been to a church service in my life."

"Why not?" I asked.

"Well," he said, "I had a bad experience with a church when I was in Junior High. My family didn't go to church, and I didn't know anything about it. But I was curious. So one Saturday afternoon, I went into this church building near my home. I didn't mean any harm, I just wanted to look around. But while I was in there, this man came up behind me. He grabbed me and accused me of trying to steal something. He called me a dirty name and he ran me out and threatened to call the police. I've never been back to church. I know it's unfair to judge the church by that one experience, but to this day, when I think of the church, I think of that man—the look on his face, his attitude, his cruel words—and I shudder."

The point is obvious: We can turn people on to the church or turn them out of the church by the way we speak.

Some years ago, when Catherine Booth died, her body was carried to a great auditorium in London. For hours and hours, people by the hundreds streamed by her casket in an outstanding display of love, affection, and gratitude. One man in that long line expressed what all were feeling that day: "She spoke to me as no one ever had before. She cared for me, and I could tell it by the way she talked to me. I was an outcast, lonely and lost. I will never forget her voice. There was something so wonderful and so meaningful about the way she spoke to you. You could feel the spirit and love of Christ in her words."

How is it with you? Are people drawn to Christ and to the Christian faith by the way you speak?

Can You Recommend Your Faith in Christ by the Way You Treat Others?

One of the most beautiful aspects of the Pentecost story is the way it is made clear that Christ is Lord and Savior for all people of all nations—Medes, Parthians, Egyptians, Romans, Asians, Elamites, and on and on it goes!

All of them are there. All of them are welcome. All of them are included. All of them are loved and treated with respect. All of them are invited to accept Christ and to be baptized in his name, "Whosoever will may come."

Several years ago, an interesting article by Lois Wyse appeared in *Good Housekeeping* magazine. It listed some bits of advice for young women considering marriage, some helpful guidelines for finding a good husband. She said there are six ways to learn everything you ever need to know about a man before you decide to marry him:

- Watch him drive in heavy traffic.
- Play tennis with him.
- Listen as he talks to his mother when he doesn't know you're listening.
- See how he treats those who serve him (waiters, ushers, maids, service station attendants, etc.).
- Notice how and for whom he spends his money.
- Look at his friends.

After sharing those six suggestions, she came up with yet another one—almost as an afterthought. "Oh, by the way," she said, "if you still can't make up your mind, then look at his shoes!" A man who keeps his shoes in good repair, she explained, generally tends to the rest of his life, too.

Did you notice the common thread here? Not counting the last one about the shoes, all the rest of these guidelines have to do with how we treat other people. I think the writer is onto something here, something very important. If you're looking for a mate or a friend, look at how that person treats other people. It is so true: The way we treat other people reveals a lot about who we are. It reveals a lot about our faith. Let me show you what I mean.

I know a man who lives in another state and claims to be very religious. Many people regard him as a man of great faith. He can quote scripture with the best of them. He can rattle off important dates in church history. He can recite the creeds eloquently. He can spout high-sounding theology in the air. But I'm not impressed, because I've seen how he treats his wife and children. I've seen how he treats his neighbors and those who work for him. He is harsh with people. He is tough and hostile and critical. He's judgmental, ill-tempered, and impatient with everyone around him.

All the outer religious fervor and activity mean nothing if we are cruel and hateful toward other people. When we show love, compassion, and kindness to others, that's when they really begin to see our faith. If you want to do good for Christ, then treat others with respect and love.

Does the way you speak bring others to Christ? And how about the way you treat other people? Does that bring them to Christ and Christian faith?

Can You Recommend Your Faith in Christ by the Way You Serve the Church?

At Pentecost, people by the thousands became Christians because they saw Simon Peter's commitment to the church. Peter was devoted to the church, and with good reason. There is no institution in the world that serves people better than the church does. There is no institution in the world that helps families more than the church does. There is no institution in the world that redeems lives like the church. There is no institution in the world that teaches love like the church. There is no institution in the world that lifts God up and inspires righteousness like the church does. There is no institution in the world that cultivates goodness like the church does.

But even more than that, the church has Jesus Christ! The world is starving to death for Jesus Christ, and we have him. We are here to share Jesus Christ with a needy world, and everything we do is for that purpose. We have worship services and Sunday-school classes, Bible-study groups and enrichment groups; we have youth groups, children's groups, singles groups, and mission-work groups; we take trips, put on dramas, play games, and present concerts; we paint houses, build clinics, feed the hungry, and help the needy—all for one purpose: so that we can share the love of Christ; so that we can tell people about him.

If you want to be a good witness for Christ, if you want to recommend your faith to others, the best thing you can do is serve the church with all your heart and soul.

Let me ask you something. Be honest now. What if every church member were just like you? What if every member served the church and supported the church just as you do? What kind of church would we have? Can you recommend your faith in Christ to others by the way you serve the church?

Can You Recommend Your Faith in Christ by the Way You Trust God?

Does your trust in God inspire others to trust God? We see this happening dramatically at Pentecost. When Simon Peter stood up to preach that day, he didn't know how it was going to turn out. He didn't know how his words would be received. Would they hear him with hope or hostility? Would they react positively or negatively? Would they fall on their knees beside him, or rise up in arms against him? Would they respond in faith and penitence, or would they try to stone him to death?

He didn't know, but he *did* know that the Holy Spirit was with him. So he did the best he could and trusted God to bring it out right—and God did! Simon Peter's confident trust enabled others to commit their lives to Christ and the church.

In Ralph Waldo Emerson's *Journal,* there is a tender section where Emerson reflects painfully on the tragic death of his little son, Waldo. In his grief, Emerson writes these words of faith: "All that I have seen teaches me to trust God for all that I have not seen."

Do you trust God like that? Do you trust God that much? God wants some good witnesses today. Will you step forward and stand tall and be one of them by the way you speak, by the way you treat others, by the way you serve the church, and by the way you trust God?

When you're a Christian, the whole world is from Missouri, saying, "Show me your Christian witness."

Chapter 8

CAN THE WORLD SEE YOUR LOVE?

*F*rom there he set out and went away to the region of Tyre. He
entered a house and did not want anyone to know he was there.
Yet he could not escape notice, but a woman whose little daughter
had an unclean spirit immediately heard about him, and she came
and bowed down at his feet. Now the woman was a Gentile, of
Syrophoenician origin. She begged him to cast the demon out of
her daughter. He said to her, "Let the children be fed first, for it is
not fair to take the children's food and throw it to the dogs." But
she answered him, "Sir, even the dogs under the table eat the
children's crumbs." Then he said to her, "For saying that, you may
go—the demon has left your daughter." So she went home, found
the child lying on the bed, and the demon gone.

—MARK 7:24-30

Sometimes it is not what we say but the way we say it
that is so important. For example, I once knew a man who
could say, "Let us pray," and make everybody in the room
angry. It was his arrogant tone of voice that irritated
people. Or think about this: A man seething with anger—
wild-eyed, vengeful, hostile, out-of-control, waving his
clenched fist in the air, screams, "I'll get those rascals if
it's the last thing I ever do!" Put that over against this: A
father who is playing hide and seek with his children says,

with a twinkle in his eye and fun in his voice, the very same thing: "I'll get those rascals if it's the last thing I ever do!" Same words, but a vast difference in meaning because of the tone of voice used.

I am so glad that we have the words of Jesus recorded in the scriptures, but how much better we could understand them if we could hear his tone of voice. That tone was probably one of the main reasons the little children wanted to get close to him. Obviously, they didn't understand all his words, but they did understand the love and kindness in his voice.

Little children, beggars, poor people, hurting people, the blind, the lame, the sick, the needy—they all were drawn to him, not only by what he said but by the way he said it. If, by some miracle, we could actually hear Jesus' words spoken in his special tone of voice, I think we would be able to understand his message and catch his spirit so much better.

This is uniquely the case in this perplexing and somewhat disturbing story in Mark 7, where the Greek mother comes to Jesus for help. Her daughter is sick. She has heard about Jesus and his power to heal. So as a loving, concerned parent, she comes to Jesus, kneels before him, and asks him to heal her daughter. Jesus' reply is where the story gets tricky.

I think the confusion resides in the fact that we cannot hear Jesus' tone of voice. When we look only at the stark words in black and white on the printed page, it does seem—at first glance—that Jesus is being harsh with the woman. He says, "Let the children first be fed, for it is not right to take the children's bread and throw it to the dogs."

What in the world does that mean? Well, the word "children" refers to the Jews, the children of Israel, and the word "dogs" refers to the Gentiles. The Jews regarded the Gentiles as "unclean people," and one of their most popular terms of contempt for the Gentiles was the word "dogs"—meaning the wild dogs of the street, the unclean stray dogs that roam the gutters, alleyways, and garbage dumps. But interestingly, in the original Greek, Jesus did not use the insulting word meaning "dogs." Rather, he used a diminutive word, which described not the wild, filthy dogs of the street, but the little pet dogs of the house—the family's beloved puppies. "In Greek, diminutives are characteristically affectionate. Jesus took the sting out of the word" (Barclay, *The Gospel of Mark*, p. 179). When he did that, the woman realized immediately that she was with a friend.

The woman was a Greek, and the Greeks had the gift of conversation—a love for banter, discussion, repartee, debate, mental sparring. She sensed at once in Jesus' words and tone that he was speaking with a smile, that it was a friendly dialogue, that help was on the way.

More than that, he was treating her with a respect not often given to women in those days. Men didn't discuss theological issues with women back then. Women were treated as inferior, as mindless things to be used, as chattel to be owned. But here Jesus honors her by including her in a philosophical discussion—the kind that was so important in the Greek world of old.

Leonard Griffith, in *Encounters with Christ,* talks about our Lord's deep respect for women:

> Jesus encountered a number of women during his earthly ministry, and his conduct toward them appears all the more remarkable when you remember the inferior status of woman in the first-century world. The hard Roman treated her as a slave or a plaything. The cultured Greek did not regard her as the intellectual equal of any man. Even the devout Jew listed her as an item of property along with his fields and cattle and would never break the law by talking to her about religion.
>
> The coming of Jesus invested womanhood with a new honor, and motherhood with infinite sacredness. Toward

women of all races and ranks, even fallen women, Jesus
displayed a gallant courtesy, a knightly chivalry, for which
he has been well named "the greatest Gentleman of the
ages." (Leonard Griffith, *Encounters with Christ* [New
York: Harper & Row, 1965], p. 58)

It's no accident that this story comes only a few verses
after Jesus has shown that there is no distinction between
clean and unclean foods. Here in this story, he is showing
that there is no distinction between clean and unclean
people. He is showing that he came not only for the Jews,
but for the Gentiles as well. He is showing that he is not
only the Jewish Messiah, but also the Lord of Life, the
Christ for all people, and the Savior of the whole world.
The Gentiles are included. They too have a place in his
kingdom. And aren't we glad of that!

The Greek woman realizes that Jesus is befriending her,
and she skillfully rises to the occasion with a brilliant
response. She says, "I know the children are fed first, but
surely I can have the crumbs under the table which the
children have thrown away."

Jesus loved her response. He liked her spirit. Hers was
a sunny faith that would not quit, a persistent faith that
would not take "no" for an answer. Here was a mother,
with a sick child at home, who was willing to take a chance
and go out on a limb for the sake of her child.

When tested, she responded with grace and grit, with
charm and insight. Jesus was impressed. He liked her. He
liked her boldness and her commitment to her child. And
he answered her prayer: "You have answered well. And
now you may go your way because your daughter has been
made whole."

The Greek woman returned home quickly and found
that her mission had been accomplished. Just as Jesus had
said, her daughter was completely healed. The illness was
totally gone. He had indeed made her well!

This is a fascinating story, and at this point we could go in a number of different directions. We could look at the power of Jesus to heal or the impact of the woman's bold persistence. Or we could talk about how the Greek woman symbolizes all the Gentiles and their inclusion in God's kingdom. Instead, let me invite you to look with me at the poignant portrait of love painted here. In this Greek mother's encounter with Jesus, we see three of the most important ways to express love.

We Express Love with Words

First, love can be expressed with words. The Greek woman came to Jesus that day to express in words her love for her sick child. What's more, in the whole Gospel of Mark, she is the only person who lovingly calls Jesus "Lord."

It seems that it would be so easy to express our love with words, but the truth is that precious few people do it well. Why is that? Why do we have trouble speaking the words of love? If we only realized how powerful words are, I think we would work harder at the task of expressing our love with words.

Some years ago, an elderly woman in her eighties was dying in a local hospital. Her son flew in to be with her. I happened to be present when he arrived and entered the room. He walked over to the bedside of his aged and dying mother, leaned over, and kissed her on the cheek.

Then, touched by that tender moment of seeing her so weak and vulnerable, he said, "Mom, you have been such a good mother to me. And I want you to know I love you."

Through tears, she said, "Son, that's the first time you've ever told me. Last Friday was your sixty-third birthday, and that's the first time you ever told me." It took him sixty-three years to say, "I love you" to his mother.

Let me ask you something. Is there a word of love you need to speak today? If you are fortunate enough to still have your parents, how long has it been since you told your mom or dad how much you love them and appreciate them? Or if you are married, how long has it been since you told your mate? I don't mean a quick, routine, matter-of-fact "I love you," but a real heart-to-heart expression of your love in words.

And if you are a parent, how long has it been since you told your children how proud you are of them and how much you cherish them? Let me suggest something. For one week, write down every word you say to your children, and then ask yourself: How many of these words are words of love, encouragement, and appreciation—not just words of correction or discipline? I know that as parents, sometimes we need to be referees, and that is a loving thing to do. But also we need to be cheerleaders. We need to say "I love you."

There is no question about it. One of the best ways to express love is with words.

We Express Love with Attitude

We can express our love with our attitude toward life. One of the things about the Greek woman that impressed Jesus most was her attitude. She was committed to her child, and she was willing to do whatever it took to get help for her sick daughter. She was bold, persistent, and courageous because she lived by the attitude of love. She would not be put off. She would not be discouraged. She would not give up, because she lived by the attitude of love.

Some years ago in a mining town in West Virginia, a seventeen-year-old boy took a summer job in the coal mines. Being a "coal miner" for the summer sounded adventuresome and macho. The second week on the job, however, the boy became lost deep down in the mine. He had been working with a group of veteran miners who had warned and cautioned him. They had told him to stay close to the group, because it would be so easy to get lost down in the numerous caves and treacherous passageways.

But one day he absent-mindedly wandered away from his workteam and became completely lost! He yelled for help, but the miners had moved on to another location and did not hear him. Then suddenly his light went out, and he was in total darkness. He was absolutely terrified and began to cry. He thought, "This is how it all ends for me. I'm going to die down here. I don't know which way to go. I don't know how to get out," and he dropped on his knees to pray.

"O God, help me!" he said out loud. "O God, please help me!" Then he noticed something. As he was kneeling there to pray, he felt his knee touching something hard. It was a railroad track. He realized that if he followed that track, it would lead him out!

And that's what he did. He followed the track, and eventually it brought him out of the dark depths of the mine to light and safety.

That's a parable for us, isn't it? If we will hold onto the track of love and follow wherever it leads, if we will make love our attitude in life, no matter how dark some moments may be, the love-track will bring us out and lead us to the light.

As much as it may sound like a cliche, it is still profoundly true: "Love is the answer." We would do well to hold onto that track and live by that attitude. As Christians, it is our calling to live always by the spirit and attitude of love. We can express our love with attitude.

We Express Love with Actions

That Greek mother in Mark 7 put her love to work. She acted it out. She expressed her love with actions. How important that is!

I went to college with a girl from Sarawak, Borneo. Her grandfather had been a headhunter. One night when she was in high school, she went to a youth program led by a Methodist college student. That night she was converted. She accepted Christ as her Savior and dedicated her life to him.

But then she had a problem. How would she tell her parents about her newfound faith? She decided not to tell them in words, but rather to show them in deeds of love. Here's how she described what happened:

> Before Christ came into my life, I was spoiled and selfish. I was irritable and impatient. I was disrespectful to my parents. My room was a mess, and my attitude was worse. But after Christ came into my life, I changed. I was kind to my parents. I cleaned up my room. I helped with the housework. I spoke with tenderness and respect to my parents. I was loving toward everyone.
>
> My parents noticed, and they said to me, "Daughter, you are different! Why? What has happened to you?"
>
> I said to them, "Yes, I am different. I have been reborn! I have Christ as my Savior. I am a Christian now, and Christians always live by the law of love."
>
> And my parents said, "Tell us more of this religion. Tell us more of this Christ. If he can change people like that, we want to be Christians, too!"

Well, that's the way it works. We can express our love with words, with attitude, and—most powerfully, dramatically, and meaningfully—with actions!

When you're a Christian, the whole world is from Missouri, saying, "Show me your love."

Chapter 9

CAN THE WORLD SEE YOUR BIGNESS OF SPIRIT?

I *f you love those who love you, what credit is that to you? For even sinners love those who love them. If you do good to those who do good to you, what credit is that to you? For even sinners do the same. If you lend to those from whom you hope to receive, what credit is that to you? Even sinners lend to sinners, to receive as much again. But love your enemies, do good, and lend, expecting nothing in return. Your reward will be great, and you will be children of the Most High; for he is kind to the ungrateful and the wicked. Be merciful, just as your Father is merciful."*

—LUKE 6:32-36

Some years ago, there was a highly respected minister in Louisiana, Dr. F. M. Freeman, who served as pastor of some of the finest churches in the state. He was greatly appreciated and deeply loved by both ministers and lay people. He also was a delightful man, known for his quick wit and great sense of humor.

When he was well up in his eighties, he had a conversation one day with a young minister.

Dr. Freeman said, "I want to tell you something, and I want you to remember this all of your life: Never, never hate anybody!"

The young minister replied, "I agree with you, Dr. Freeman. I agree with you completely."

Dr. Freeman continued, "Now listen closely. Take this deep into your soul. I'm not saying this casually. I mean it with all my heart. Do not allow yourself to hate anyone. Life is too short for that!"

The young minister agreed with him again.

Then Dr. Freeman said, "Don't hate anyone. Life is too short for that. I have followed that advice all of my life."

And then, with a twinkle in his eye, he patted his shirt pocket and said, "But I do carry this list around with me, so if I ever backslide, I'll know right where I'm going to start!"

Of course, Dr. Freeman was only kidding with that last comment. Anyone who knew him found him to be a kind, loving, gracious person who truly understood that life is too short for things such as hostility, hatred, vengeance, littleness, and grudges. He knew that those things are spiritual poisons that will absolutely devastate our souls. You and I know where he learned that, don't we? Of course we do. He learned it from Jesus!

In the opening verses from Luke 6, Jesus essentially was saying in that sermon on the plain, "Life is too short for hatred and vengeance and grudges and malice and resentment and self-pity. We don't need to give in to those toxic attitudes. We don't need to live that way. With God as our helper, we can choose the way of love and grace and forgiveness."

Earlier in this century, a woman went to her doctor one day with a catalogue of complaints about her health. The physician examined her thoroughly and became convinced that nothing physical was wrong with her. He suspected that her problem was her negative outlook on life, her bitterness, her resentment, her grudges, and her self-pity. Every day for her was another "woe-is-me pity party," another day to nurse her grievances, feel sorry for herself, and become more and more angry about how, in her mind, she had been mistreated by people and by life in general.

The wise physician took her into a backroom in his office where he kept some of his medicine. He showed her a shelf filled with empty bottles and said to her, "See those bottles. Notice that all of them are empty. They are shaped differently, but basically, they are all alike. And most important, they have nothing in them."

"Now," he said, "I can take one of these bottles and fill it with poison—enough poison to kill a human being. Or I could take the same bottle and fill it with medicine—enough medicine . . . to bring down a fever, or ease a throbbing headache, or fight bacteria in one part of the body."

"The important thing is," said the doctor, "that I make the choice. I can fill it with whatever I choose. I can fill it with poison that will hurt or with medicine that will heal."

Then the doctor looked the woman straight in the eye and said, "Each day that God gives us is basically like one of those empty bottles. We can choose to fill it with love and life-affirming thoughts and attitudes that lift us and other people up, or we can fill it with destructive poisonous thoughts that pull us, and everyone we meet, down. The choice is ours" (*Homiletics* Jan./March 1994, pp.8-9).

What will we choose? How will we fill our days? In Luke 6, Jesus gives us the answer. He wants us to spend our days imitating the gracious, loving, merciful, healing Spirit of God. Isn't this another way of saying, "Life is too short for littleness and self-pity; life is too short for hate and grudges and quarreling; life is too short for resentment and jealousies; life is too short for anything less than love"?

Let me explore this further by suggesting three things we must remember as we concentrate on the urgency and quickness of life today.

Life Is Too Short for Pettiness

Pettiness can cut us off from God, from other people, and from the church. Please don't let that happen to you.

I am thinking of a man in another state who is a great singer. He has an outstanding tenor voice, but he has not sung in church for many years. Twenty-three years ago, he was active in his church's music program, sang in the choir, and was the church's main soloist. But then he went to a convention in New York, and there he discovered that some of the large churches in New York City pay their choir members. So when he returned home, he gave his church an ultimatum: "Pay me or I quit the choir!"

The church declined his offer, and he quit. The choir suffered his loss for a while, but soon enough, others came along to take his place. You see, none of us is indispensable. The church rolls on.

That man has sulked for twenty-three years. He doesn't come to church much anymore, and when he does come, he sits in the congregation with bitterness written all over his face. He is mad most of the time. He is cynical and critical of the church, especially the music program, but people long ago stopped listening to him.

Here is a man who has wasted his talent—and has wasted twenty-three years. Think of what he has missed while making himself miserable through pettiness!

Life is too short for littleness, and pettiness is such a waste of time and talent and energy.

Life Is Too Short for Hurt Feelings

Hurt feelings can cut us off from God, from other people, and from the church. Please don't let that happen to you.

I'm thinking of a woman who quite suddenly quit the church. When the pastor asked her why, she said, "My sister passed away on September 20, and I didn't get a sympathy card from my Sunday-school class until October 3! I will never forgive the church or that class for slighting me like that!"

I wonder what Jesus would say to her. I wonder what the apostle Paul would say. My guess is they would say to her, "Come on now! Life is too short for that! Life is too short for pettiness and hurt feelings. They are such a waste."

Life Is Too Short for Bitterness and Ill Will

Bitterness and ill will can contaminate the soul, cutting us off from God, from other people, and from the church. Please don't let that happen to you.

I'm thinking of a couple who became upset with their church in the early 1960s because of a social decision the church made. The couple became sick with bitterness and hostility. It was all they could talk about. At every meal, they fussed about the church. Each evening in the den, they harshly criticized the church and its leaders. They wrote angry, hot letters, complaining about the church. They looked constantly for materials to use against the church. And they made abusive speeches blasting the church.

This went on for five years, and their children looked on and listened and took it all in. Finally, their hostility spent, the couple decided to go back to the church. But they ran into something they hadn't counted on. Their children didn't want to have anything to do with the church now. Strangely enough, that couple couldn't understand that. For five years, they had bitterly denounced the church in front of their children because of one decision the church's board had made, and inadvertently, they had taught their children to hate the church and its people.

Five years of bitterness. Five years of hostility. Five years of ill will. How do you undo that? How do you correct it? Is it too late? One thing is sure: Life is too short for bitterness and ill will! It is so dangerous and so harmful. It is a waste of time and energy—and sometimes a waste of young lives.

"Ill will"—that's a phrase that means a lot of things and covers a multitude of sins. Jealousy, envy, resentment, grudge-bearing, vengeance, stubborn pride, haughtiness, spite, hatred—all these are what we mean by "ill will," and nothing is more spiritually draining. Ill will is a fitting name for them, because they are all sick!

Christ came to bring wholeness, to make us well, to heal us, to deliver us from all these sins of ill will. Isn't that what conversion is? Christ coming into our lives and changing our ill will to goodwill!

I once read about a lady who phoned her TV service-man and complained that something was wrong with her set. The serviceman asked if there were any visible symptoms.

"Well, the newscast is on right now," said the lady, "and the reporter has a very long face."

The serviceman replied, "Lady, if you had to report what's happening these days, you'd have a long face too!"

I know that in this world today, there are a lot of things that tend to drive us to ill will and a long face. But I also know that a "faith adjustment" can make all the difference in how we view the world and how we relate to it. You see, we have only so much energy, and broadly speaking, it can be used in one of two ways: for good or ill—to build up or tear down; to do the things of love or the things of hate.

Interestingly, both goodwill and ill will, both love and hate, are like boomerangs. Whichever you send out will come back. If you give love, it comes back to bless you. If you give hate, it comes back to haunt you.

The real truth is that life is just too short for bitterness and ill will. It's too short for grudges and quarrels and spite and prejudice and hatred. All these can cut us off not only from people, but also from God!

Now, be honest for a moment. What about you? Are you letting some miserable misunderstanding keep you constantly tense and spiritually drained? Are you feeling some jealousy or resentment? Are you keeping some quarrel alive? Are you holding a grudge? Do you need to say "I'm sorry" or "Forgive me" or "I love you"? If so, then now is the time to swallow your pride and set it right! Now is the time to do something about it! Don't let the sun go down tonight before you have fixed it. Tomorrow may be too late. Life is so quickly passed. It is much too brief to give time and energy to "littleness." We were made in the image of God and meant to be "big." Life is too short for anything less.

When you're a Christian, the whole world is from Missouri, saying, "Show me your bigness of spirit."

Chapter 10

CAN THE WORLD SEE YOUR KINSHIP TO GOD?

*T*hen *his mother and his brothers came; and standing outside, they sent to him and called him. A crowd was sitting around him; and they said to him, "Your mother and your brothers and sisters are outside, asking for you." And he replied, "Who are my mother and my brothers?" And looking at those who sat around him, he said, "Here are my mother and my brothers! Whoever does the will of God is my brother and sister and mother."*

—MARK 3:31-35

Have you heard the story about the woman in Birmingham who came upon a small boy in the downtown area of the city one January morning? The little boy, who looked to be eight or nine years old, was obviously from a poor family. His clothes were frayed and threadbare, and he was barefoot! He had no shoes or socks, and it was a bitter cold morning. Snow was swirling in the air, and the store windows were frosted over.

Trying to find relief from the cold, the little boy was standing with his bare feet on the grating of a hot-air vent outside a bakery. The warm air felt good as it curled around his toes, but still he was shivering in the frigid wind. As the woman walked up to him, she saw immediately how cold he was. And when her eyes fell on his chapped, bare feet, her heart went out to him.

She was moved to compassion as she said, "Son, it's way below freezing this morning! Where on earth are your shoes?"

"Don't have any," he answered.

"Well, we will see about that," she said.

She took him by the hand, and they walked to a nearby department store. She bought him a new pair of shoes, several pair of socks, and a new warm winter coat. When they came out of the store, he was so proud of his new gifts that he ran off down the sidewalk toward home to show his family his good fortune. When he had covered about thirty yards, however, suddenly he screeched to a stop, turned around, and ran back to the woman.

His face was beaming as he said, "Lady, I almost forgot to thank you for my shoes and socks and coat."

"You are more than welcome," she answered.

"Also, Ma'am," he said, "I wanted to ask you something. Are you God's wife?"

That question threw her for a moment. She blushed and stumbled for an answer, and then she said with a smile, "No, I am not God's wife, but I am one of his children!"

The little boy replied, "I knew it! I knew it! I just knew you were some kin to him!"

That story raises a poignant and pointed question: Can people look at us today and tell that we are kin to God? Can people look at the way we act, the way we talk, the way we behave, the way we treat others, the way we support the church, and tell that we are kin to God? Can people spend a few minutes with us and know by our values and our commitments and our compassion that we are, without question, God's kinfolks?

Be honest now. Can people see the Spirit of God in *you?* Can they sense in you the Spirit of Christ? Can they tell that you are related to God? Jesus put it like this: "Whoever does the will of God is my brother and sister and mother." Think about that. Is commitment to the will of

God dramatic and prominent and vital in your life? Are you so committed to doing the will of God that people can look at you and know immediately that you are one of God's kinfolks?

To bring this closer to home, let me raise three questions for you to think about seriously.

Can People Tell by the Way You Live That You Are Kin to God?

Some time ago, a little girl in our church asked me to come and watch her play soccer. I went, and as I sat in the stands at the soccer game, an interesting thing happened. Just before the teams took the field, a little girl on the opposing team ran up to the woman seated next to me and said to her, "Will you hold my watch and money for me while I'm playing?" The woman smiled and said she would be glad to take good care of her things.

After the game, the little girl returned to retrieve her valuables. The woman said to her, "I want to ask you something. Why me? Out of all these people, why did you pick me to hold your watch and money?"

"Because of that," the little girl said. She was pointing to the cross the woman was wearing on her necklace. "Since you were wearing a cross—and also because I saw you being nice to your children out in the parking lot before the game—I knew you were a Christian, and I knew I could trust you!"

Can people see the sign of the cross in your life? In the way you live? In the way you act? In the way you speak? I'm not talking about jewelry. It's fine to wear the symbols of faith like a cross or a fish or a dove or an angel, but the more important question is: Can people see the sign of the cross, the Spirit of Christ, the will of God, in the way you live?

It is good and helpful to have people who can preach eloquent and stirring sermons, or sing beautiful solos, or teach inspiring lessons. But the most powerful and effective way to share the Christian faith and show our kinship to God is to live it every day. Poet Edgar Guest put it succinctly in "Sermons We See":

> I may misunderstand you and the high advice you give,
> But there's no misunderstanding how you act and how you live.

It's an important question to grapple with honestly: Can people tell by the way you live that you are kin to God?

Can People Tell by the Way You Laugh That You Are Kin to God?

Some people go miserably through life crying, "Woe is me," "Poor me," at every turn. How sad that is, because God meant life to be full, vibrant, abundant, joyous, and sprinkled with laughter. Can you imagine what it would be like to live in a humorless world? A good healthy sense of humor is a gift from God. As someone has said, if you have any doubts that God has a sense of humor, just go look in a mirror!

Abraham Lincoln once said, "If I did not laugh from time to time, I would surely die." We should learn not to take ourselves so seriously. We should learn to lighten up and laugh. After all, our faith is full of joy and gladness. Why, the very word *gospel* (*evangelion* in the Greek of the New Testament) means "good news," "glad tidings."

The guest speaker at one of the men's breakfasts at our church was Clark Kent Ervin. Clark, who happens to be an African American, is one of the bright young leaders of Houston. He grew up in the Third Ward in Houston and went on to distinguish himself at Harvard University and Law School. He has practiced law with some of the finest firms in the nation.

When Clark was in his late twenties, he was asked by then President George Bush to come to Washington to help develop the President's "Thousand Points of Light" program. One morning as Clark was preparing to leave Houston and take up his new job as part of the White House staff, the phone rang. Clark was told that it was *Time* magazine on the line.

Clark said, "I wasn't surprised. After all, I was going to Washington, and evidently *Time* had heard about me and wanted to interview me."

Clark told his secretary to tell them he was not available at the moment, but to please call back in five minutes. Clark wanted some time to think of some quotable quotes that would be catchy and poignant, that might resound across the ages. Exactly five minutes later *Time* called back, and Clark was ready with his brilliant quotes. He had them written down. This conversation took place:

"Is this Clark Ervin?"

"Yes."

"Is this Clark Kent Ervin?"

"Yes."

"Well, this is *Time* magazine calling, and we just wanted to know if you would like to renew your subscription."

What's great about that humorous story is that Clark Kent Ervin takes great delight in telling it on himself. He is able to laugh at himself, and that is wholesome.

It bothers me that so many professional comedians these days really misunderstand humor. They are so insecure that they think profane language and gutter talk is the only way to make people laugh. Or they resort to bashing and crucifying other people in the name of humor. The really great comedians know better. They know that the best humor is a good laugh at ourselves. Will Rogers, Jack Benny, Lucille Ball, Johnny Carson, and Red Skelton were great because they helped us laugh at ourselves, not take ourselves too seriously. They helped us lighten up.

Think about this: What makes you laugh? Profanity?
Derisive and cruel put-downs of other people? Jokes that
ridicule groups or nationalities or races? Hurtful jibes that
take advantage of someone else's misfortune? Do you find
those things funny? Do they make you laugh? I hope not.
Laughter at someone else's expense is not Christian. The
best humor is a good laugh at ourselves! And the best
laughter is that which comes not from someone's misfortune, but from someone's good fortune.

Can people tell by the way you laugh that you are kin
to God?

Can People Tell by the Way You Love That You Are Kin to God?

Do you remember those wonderful lines from the great
Broadway musical "My Fair Lady," when Eliza Doolittle
turns to Professor Higgins and sings:

> Don't talk of stars burning above,
> If you're in love, show me.

In a way, this is what the world is saying to us today:
Don't just talk of faith . . .
Don't just talk of hope . . .
Don't just talk of goodness . . .
Don't just talk of God . . .
Show me! Show me with your love!

Jesus called love the key sign of discipleship and kinship with God. In John 13, he reminds us that "they'll
know we are Christians by our love."

Well, what do you think? Be honest, now. Can people
tell by the way you live, the way you laugh, and the way
you love that you are kin to God?

When you're a Christian, the whole world is from
Missouri, saying, "Show me your kinship to God."

Chapter 11

CAN THE WORLD SEE YOUR STRENGTH IN FACING STRESS?

*A*t that time Jesus said, "I thank you, Father, Lord of heaven and earth, because you have hidden these things from the wise and the intelligent and have revealed them to infants; yes, Father, for such was your gracious will. All things have been handed over to me by my Father; and no one knows the Son except the Father, and no one knows the Father except the Son and anyone to whom the Son chooses to reveal him. Come to me, all you that are weary and are carrying heavy burdens, and I will give you rest. Take my yoke upon you, and learn from me; for I am gentle and humble in heart, and you will find rest for your souls. For my yoke is easy, and my burden is light."

—MATTHEW 11:25-30

One Sunday morning, a mother said to her ten-year-old son, "Billy, I'm not feeling well enough to go to church today, but I want you to go on as usual. Then you can tell me all about it."

Obediently, Billy carried out his mom's wish. When he returned home, his mother asked, "Well, Billy, how was church?"

"Fine," Billy responded.

"Where did you sit?" she asked.

"Oh, I think I sat in about the same place we always sit." Billy's answer was just vague enough to make his mother suspicious.

"What was the sermon about?" she asked.

Again, as ten-year-old boys will, Billy fumbled a bit for an answer, and finally said, "Oh . . . uh . . . Let's see . . . oh yes, I remember now. It was something about 'Keep your shirt on and you will get a blanket.' "

That did it. Billy's mother called the pastor and asked him about the text for the sermon.

He answered, "Be patient, and the Comforter will come!"

Actually, that's a pretty good verse to remember these days, because we live in a tough and tense world that often "stresses us to the max."

As my good friend Rod Wilmoth put it, "We're all stressed up with no place to blow!" Desperately, we need the strength and comfort that God alone can give.

A few years ago, the Comprehensive Care Corporation of Tampa, Florida, published a booklet about stress in our modern world. The facts are disturbing:

1. One out of four (that's 25 percent of the American people) suffers from mild to moderate depression, anxiety, loneliness, and other painful symptoms attributed mainly to stress.
2. Four out of five adult family members see a need for less stress in their daily lives.
3. Approximately half of all diseases can be linked to stress-related origins, including ulcers, colitis, bronchial asthma, high blood pressure, and some forms of cancer.
4. Unmanaged stress is a leading factor in homicides, suicides, child abuse, spouse abuse, and other aggravated assaults.
5. The problem of stress is taking a tremendous toll economically, also. In our nation alone, we Americans are now spending 64.9 billion dollars a year trying to deal with the issue of stress.

I share these sobering statistics for three reasons: (1) to help us see the size of the problem; (2) to help us see that if we are experiencing stress-related problems, we are not alone; (3) and most important, to remind us that there is hope. When we feel stressed-out, there is help and comfort and healing and peace for our troubled souls.

Jesus shared the "good news" with us a long time ago when he said, "Come to me, all you that are weary and are carrying heavy burdens, and I will give you rest." In other words, "Come to me all who are exhausted and stressed-out, and I will give you peace and comfort and strength." We have the answer in our hands. We've had it all along. Yet too often, we look for help in all the wrong places.

There is a story about a farmer who went to a government bureaucrat who specialized in animal health. The farmer sought help from the "expert" because ten of his chickens had suddenly and unexplainably died. The government expert instructed the farmer to give aspirin to all the surviving chickens.

Two days later, however, the farmer returned. Twenty more chickens had died. What should he do now? The expert said quickly, "Give all the rest castor oil."

Two days later, the farmer returned a third time and reported thirty more dead chickens. The government expert now strongly recommended penicillin.

Two days later, a very sad farmer returned. All the rest of his chickens had now died. They were all gone.

"What a shame," said the expert. "I have lots more remedies!"

The world offers many so-called remedies for the problem of stress, but the truth is that most of them don't work. The world offers many so-called experts on stress management, but the truth is that there is only one Great Physician who can give us the comfort and strength we need. The world offers many so-called solutions for the tensions and burdens that push us down and pull us apart, but the truth is that there is only one Prince of Peace who can soothe our jangled nerves and save our troubled souls. There is only One who can truthfully say, "Come to me, all of you who are exhausted and weary and worn and troubled and stressed-out, and I will give you rest; I will give you comfort; I will give you the strength you need for the living of these days."

As you walk along the rural roads of India, every now and then you will come to a post about shoulder high with a strong shelf on top of it. These posts are called "Soma Tonga," which means "resting place." People who walk the roads carrying loads on their backs can stop at a Soma Tonga, place their heavy load on the shelf, and rest a while before continuing their journey. It is not surprising that new believers in India call Christ "My Soma Tonga"—the One who gives me rest, the One who takes my burden, the One who renews my strength.

Sadly, often in this world too many of us forget that Christ is our strength. Sometimes when we feel stressed-out, we rush out in desperation to chase after every new fad that comes along, every new guru who promises a quick-fix for our problems.

Over the years, I have noticed that, broadly speaking, people try to deal with their stress in three ways—three basically different philosophies about how we should handle stress:

1. Escape the stress.
2. Endure the stress.
3. Elevate the stress.

Let's take a look at these one at a time and see if we can find ourselves somewhere between the lines.

Some Say, "Escape the Stress"

"Stress is bad," these people say, "so avoid it at all costs." Get away. Run away. Fly away. Take a pill to ease your nerves. Take a drink to drown your sorrows. Take a shot to kill the pain. Get drunk, take drugs, sleep a lot. Do whatever you have to do to escape the stress. That's what this first school of thought says to us. It's not a good answer to the problem of stress, but it is a popular one these days. If you want to verify that, watch TV commercials and notice how many of them advocate this escape philosophy. They brag about it. They have just the right drink, just the right pill, just the right place, just the right trip to solve all your problems by getting you away from them.

Now, please don't misunderstand me. I know that there are times when it's appropriate and helpful to take medicine or go on vacation or retreat and get away from it all for a while, but that's not what I'm talking about. I'm talking about the escapism approach to life, rooted in the mistaken notion that all stress is bad, that the overriding task in life is to escape from the stress—to run away and hide from the problems and pressures and demands and challenges of life.

Some years ago, I was asked to be the master of ceremonies at a teenage beauty pageant. I saw something in that experience that broke my heart. A stage-door mom was filling her teenage daughter with tranquilizers. Before every event, the mother would say to her daughter, "Here, take one of these. It will calm you down." She must have given her close to twenty pills over that two-day pageant.

Finally I said to that mother, "I don't mean to interfere, but do you think it's a good idea to give your daughter so many tranquilizers?"

The mom said, "Oh, you don't understand. She has to have them. She is so weak and fragile, I must protect her.

She just can't handle any kind of stress without these miracle pills. They are just wonderful!"

By the time the pageant was over, that teenage girl was walking and moving and talking like a zombie. And at the end, her mother felt she had to give her some other kinds of pills to "cheer her up" because she didn't win. Isn't that tragic? Isn't that sad? I felt so sorry for that young girl, and I shudder to think of what might have happened to her in the years that followed.

Now, that mother would have been the first to "shrink back in horror" at the very thought of drug abuse or child abuse, but look what she was doing to her daughter—what she was teaching her. She was saying to her, "You are weak and frail and fragile and nervous and inadequate, and you can't make it in this life without drugs." She was repeatedly drilling that message into her daughter's soul with words and actions and body language and tranquilizers, because her escapism philosophy of life was rooted in the false notion that all stress is bad and should be avoided.

This is a classic example of the first approach to stress—escape the stress—and as we have seen, this escapism mind-set has many weaknesses and problems.

Others Say, "Endure the Stress"

One day I was driving on an old dirt road way out in the country when I came to a sign: "Be real careful which ruts you get into. You'll be in them for the next twenty miles!" Some people get in the rut of seeing life as nothing more than just coping, just enduring, just surviving, just sticking it out.

In a "Peanuts" cartoon, Charlie Brown expressed it like this: "I have a new philosophy of life, Linus. From this moment on, I'm going to dread only one day at a time!"

That's a light treatment of a very serious subject. Many people today do see life as a daily "grind," a hard grueling test to be endured. But where's the joy? Where's the zest? Where's the enthusiasm? Where's the excitement? For these people, the celebration of life faded and died long ago. Life for them is now drudgery. They cope, they withstand, they persist, they bear up. But surely God meant life to be more than an endurance test. Life is God's wonderful gift to us—even with all its stresses and problems and pressures. God wants our lives to be full, meaningful, abundant, creative, productive, joyful.

In addition to being a gifted writer, Robert Raines also directs a retreat center up in the beautiful Pocono Mountains in northern Pennsylvania. Early one morning some years ago, he got into his car and started driving through the mountains. There was no one on the road at that time as the mountains were quietly beginning a new day. The beautiful colors of autumn were splashed all over the trees. It was a magnificent and glorious sight as the early morning sun glistened upon the wonders of the mountains and the valleys below. And then Robert Raines saw one of the most beautiful things he had ever witnessed in his life.

Right there at the very edge of that great mountain peak, facing the gorgeous valley below, was a young man in his early twenties with a trumpet pressed to his lips. Can you guess what he was playing? Expanding his lungs fully and releasing all of the energy in his soul, he was playing the Doxology on his trumpet!

> Praise God, from whom all blessings flow;
> Praise Him, all creatures here below,
> Praise Him above, ye heavenly host,
> Praise Father, Son, and Holy Ghost.

With all the stresses and problems in this life, still the truth is that we have so many Doxologies to sing, so much to be grateful for, so many blessings to count. The point is this: Life is more than a grueling endurance test. Life is more than a survival game. Life is more than a coping competition. It's not enough to just escape the stress. It's not enough to just endure the stress. Thank God there is another option.

Still Others Say, "Elevate the Stress"

In other words, do something positive with the stress in your life. Bring it to God, and God will give you the strength to turn your problems into opportunities. Don't just try to escape the stress. Don't just try to endure the stress. Elevate the stress! Let it spur you to action. Use the stress to do something good for the cause of Christ.

Let me be honest. If I were never "under stress," I would never accomplish much. I would procrastinate. I would put things off. The stress serves as a friend to me. When crunch time comes, it makes me "get with the program."

Remember the powerful words found in Matthew 11. Jesus says: "Come to me, all you who are weary and are carrying heavy burdens, and I will give you rest." Then Jesus adds: "Take my yoke upon you and learn from me." A key word here is "yoke." In a nutshell, it means "service" or "ministry." What Jesus is saying here is this: "Put service to God and others first in your life. Let that be your number-one priority, and everything else will fall in place for you." Redeeming the stress, using the stress, letting the stress stir us to creative service for God—that is a key to Christian living.

Dietrich Bonhoeffer had a stressful life. He had been captured by the Nazi Gestapo and placed in one of those horrible prison camps—as some people called them, "death camps." In that deplorable situation, he wrote these words: "O Lord, whatever this day may bring, Thy name be praised."

And how about the apostle Paul? He had been beaten and flogged and imprisoned and run out of town; he had been shipwrecked and suffered from exposure while adrift at sea; he had been stoned and robbed and scourged and criticized. Talk about stress! Yet through it all, he could say, "I'm ready for anything, for Christ is my strength." In other words, whatever you throw at me, I'm going to elevate it, use it to serve my Christ. He is my Rock. He is my Fortress. He is my Strength. He is my Lord.

Can you say that and mean it? This is our calling as Christians—not just to escape the stress or endure the stress, but to elevate the stress and use it to serve our Lord.

When you're a Christian, the whole world is from Missouri, saying, "Show me your strength in facing stress."

Chapter 12

CAN THE WORLD SEE YOUR VISION?

*T*he king that faithfully judgeth the poor, his throne shall be established for ever. The rod and reproof give wisdom: but a child left to himself bringeth his mother to shame. When the wicked are multiplied, transgression increaseth: but the righteous shall see their fall. Correct thy son, and he shall give thee rest; yea, he shall give delight unto thy soul. Where there is no vision, the people perish: but he that keepeth the law, happy is he.

—PROVERBS 29:14-18 KJV

There was a man who went to the doctor and said, "Doc, can you help me? I have pain everywhere. I hurt all over."

"What do you mean?" asked the doctor.

"Well," the man said, "It's like this. If I take my finger and touch my shoulder, it hurts. If I touch my elbow, it hurts. If I touch my knee, it hurts. If I touch my foot, it hurts. Do you have any idea what's wrong with me?"

"Of course I do," said the doctor. "You have a broken finger!"

Strange as it may sound, this silly story is a haunting parable for us today. We are hurting all over because we have broken down in one area. Since 1960, there has been a 560 percent increase in violent crime in America and a 400 percent increase in illegitimate births. There are more robberies, more murders, more break-ins, more rapes, more abortions, more abuses, more promiscuity, more profanity than ever before in our land. Everywhere we look, we see the pain, but actually it all comes from one source—from one broken finger. Since the end of World War II, we have become so permissive, so fuzzy about what is right and wrong, so wishy-washy on ethical matters, that we are in danger of losing our morality as a nation.

When I was growing up, things were very straightforward and clear-cut. I was taught early on that it's wrong to steal, cheat, lie, hurt others, hit, or be profane. Today we water it all down so quickly, excuse it so lightly, muddy it up so eloquently, and explain it away so neatly. Many people act as if the Ten Commandments are merely ten suggestions.

Some years ago, I was a guest speaker at a youth retreat. We were discussing Christian ethics, and I asked the young people, "Is it wrong to cheat in school?" Their answer was interesting, revealing, and disturbing.

They said, "It's wrong to cheat, except in Latin class."

"What do you mean? How did you come to that conclusion?" I asked.

They answered, "Well, the teacher is terrible, so it's O.K. to cheat in that class." Unfortunately, they were dead serious. They had reasoned it out, explained it away, excused it so neatly.

That kind of "moral watering down" is a small example of a much larger problem in our land: We are in danger of losing our soul as a nation. We are in danger of losing our sense of right and wrong, and we already are living with the consequences! Crime is running rampant across our land. It's a two-edged sword. On the one hand, there is violent crime, with its baggage of greed and guns, drugs and deviancy, gang warfare, and mob madness. And along with it all, there is something else that concerns me greatly: There is no cry of public outrage. Sadly, we are getting used to it!

Justice Edwin Torres, judge of the Supreme Court in New York, says, "A society that loses its sense of moral outrage is doomed to extinction." He condemns our acceptance of the unacceptable. In a letter to Senator Daniel Patrick Moynihan, he writes, "This numbness, this near narcoleptic state can diminish the human condition to the level of combat infantrymen, who, in protracted campaigns, can eat their battle-field rations . . . while seated on the dead bodies of the fallen, friend and foe alike" (*Homiletics*, Jan./Mar. 1994, p. 45).

Listen in on this conversation:

"What's going on in your neighborhood?"

"Oh, nothing unusual. Another break-in down the street. A woman was kidnapped over at the mall. A man was mugged at the grocery store. There was another gang fight on the south side, and a drive-by shooting took the life of a sleeping child. A couple was shot last week going to lunch. And the drug dealers are getting closer. Nothing unusual. Same old stuff."

How can we be silent with all this going on? Where is the cry of public moral outrage?

In 1951, 3,000 children died of polio, and we stood up and screamed, "We will not put up with that. We will not let this disease kill our children." That outcry sparked a massive, global effort to stop the epidemic, and we stopped it.

In 1991, 5,356 children—not counting the number of adults—were killed by guns. More than 5,000 children in one year—that's almost 15 a day—destroyed by guns, and we shrug it off!

The late novelist Walker Percy commented that the biggest threat to our nation is not some hostile military force, but spiritual decay within—decay "from weariness, boredom, cynicism, greed, and in the end, helplessness before its great problems." Our only hope is to turn back to God, to commit our lives to God and his righteousness. That's where we get our moral bearings. "Only when we turn our affections and desires toward the right things—toward enduring noble, spiritual things—only then will things get better." (William Bennett, "Commuter Massacre, Our Warning," *Wall Street Journal,* December 10, 1993).

When the noted artist Whistler was at the height of his artistic career, a wealthy patron bought one of his paintings on the condition that the artist would accompany him home and help select the perfect spot to hang the picture. After they arrived at his mansion, the man held up the painting first here and then there, and each time he would ask, "How about this?"

Finally, Whistler said, "You are going about this all wrong. What you must do is remove all the furnishings from the room, hang the painting where it will be best displayed, and then arrange the furniture in relationship to the painting" (Jon Allen, "24 Best Stewardship Illustrations," quoted in *Windows to Truth,* Oct/Nov/Dec 1993, p. 4).

Many people today want God to be nothing more than one of the furnishings, just one of the decorations. But the only way life will work is for God to be the central focus, the focal point of our existence. In his classic novel *Brothers Karamazov,* Dostoyevsky reminded us that if God is left out, everything is permissible. We are now seeing everything!

This is precisely what the writer of Proverbs meant in that great verse that has resounded across the ages: "Where there is no vision, the people perish" (29:18 KJV). This means that where there is no belief in God; where there is no allegiance to God and his truth; where there is no commitment to God and his commandments; where there is no hope in God, the future is bleak for a nation.

We have a lot of religious diversity in our nation. I understand and respect that. But I also know that in recent years, we have been so afraid that we might offend someone or exclude somebody if we talk about faith that we have almost excluded God. We have let the pendulum swing too far. We must swing it back.

Remember the opening analogy of the broken finger. The good news is that a broken finger can be fixed; a fractured finger can be healed. God is the Great Physician, and if we will follow his directives, we can be his people of vision. Let's bring this closer to home by looking together at this powerful verse in Proverbs 29. Let me paraphrase this great verse in three different ways, in the hope that this will clarify for us what the word *vision* means for us today.

Where There Is No Morality, the People Perish

Morality—this is what the writer of Proverbs is talking about. If we are not committed to righteousness and goodness and justice, we are in big trouble.

William Bennett, former secretary of education in the Republican administration, wrote a powerful article for the *Wall Street Journal* that called for our nation to return to morality. He said:

> That it took a shower of bullets in a suburban railway car to outrage us is a measure of our complacency about crime and violence in our society. For too long we have allowed the deeper problems that underlie violence and other social ills to pass without comment. . . . There are places where virtue is taught and learned. But there is a lot less of this than there ought to be. . . . There is a coarseness, a callousness, a cynicism . . . and a vulgarity to our time. . . .
>
> In my view the real crisis today is spiritual. Specifically, our problem is what the ancients called *acedia* or sloth.

Acedia reveals itself as an undue concern for external affairs and worldly things. It is spiritual torpor; an absence of zeal for divine things. . . .

Material gains will not be enough here. If we . . . have cities of gold and alabaster but our children have not learned how to walk in goodness, justice, and mercy, then we will have failed. . . . As individuals and as a society, we need to return religion to its proper place. Religion, after all, provides us with moral bearings. (December 10, 1993)

Just a few days after that article came out, Hodding Carter, who represents the other end of the political pole, wrote a syndicated column applauding Bennett for what he had said and joining him in calling our nation back to morality (*Houston Post,* December 22, 1993).

They were both right: A nation built on a firm foundation of righteousness can withstand any storm and any challenge.

Leadership Magazine (Winter 1993) carried a fascinating story about the destruction of Hurricane Andrew. After the hurricane hit, a TV news crew went to southern Florida to film the widespread destruction. In one neighborhood, they found every house but one totally destroyed. Only one house had withstood the storm!

The owner was cleaning up the yard when a reporter asked him, "Sir, why is your house the only one standing? How did you manage to escape the severe damage of the hurricane?"

The man said, "I built this house myself. I built it according to the Florida state building code. When the code called for 2 x 6 roof trusses, I used 2 x 6 roof trusses. I was told that a house built according to code would withstand a hurricane. I did and it did. I suppose no one else around here followed the code."

When we follow God's moral code, we too—as individuals and as a nation—can withstand any storm. But if we don't build on the solid foundation of righteousness and justice and goodness and morality, the storms of life will simply overwhelm us.

Where There Is No Hope, the People Perish

The word *vision* in Proverbs 29 means "morality," and it also means "hope." We know this is true: We can't live without hope. We can't live without dreams. If we trust God and have confidence in him, we can do amazing things. Even though I have tried to lay out the problem, I want you to know that I am not pessimistic about the future of our nation. No, I am tremendously optimistic, for two reasons.

For one thing, we have the troublemakers outnumbered. If you placed all the people of America in a line, then pulled out the ones who are causing the violence and the hurt and the pain, that group of troublemakers would represent a very small percentage of the population. Most people want safe streets and safe neighborhoods. Most people want justice and decency. We just need to start standing up and speaking out.

The other reason I'm hopeful and optimistic is because I am a Christian. I believe in God, and I believe with all my heart that ultimately, God and righteousness will win the day.

A few years ago, a visiting professor from the University of Moscow arrived in Washington, D.C. He was interviewed by an American newspaper reporter. Among other things, he said that "religion in Russia was virtually dead." "There is no one in the churches," he said, "except a few little old ladies." It is likely that what has happened in the Soviet Union over the past few years has caused that professor to reassess the significance of those "little old ladies"!

As it turned out, those "little old ladies" knew more about what was going on in this world than the people at the Kremlin or the University of Moscow. Lenin is gone. Stalin is gone. The "little old ladies" won. By the grace of God, they won. I am convinced that what sustained them was their abiding hope that the transforming resurrection power of God was very present in them, and that nothing—no "ism," no political system, no military dictator, nobody—could ever defeat God's purposes (*Windows to Truth*, Jan/Feb/Mar 1994).

Where there is no hope, the people perish. We cannot live without hope.

Where There Is No Love, the People Perish

One of the great moments of this century occurred when Malcolm Muggeridge resigned as Rector of the University of Edinburgh in January 1958. He resigned because he would not be a party to the relaxation of rules which permitted students to buy and sell marijuana on campus. Facing a booing, hostile crowd, Muggeridge addressed the students:

> The students of this university are the beneficiaries of centuries of selfless scholarship. You are supposed to spearhead progress and to carry on the torch of humanity. . . .
>
> But how infinitely sad . . . that the form of your rebellion should be a demand for drugs, for the most tenth-rate sort of self-indulgence ever known in history. All is prepared for a release of new life. We await great works of art, the spirit of adventure and courage, and what do we get from you? Self-centered folly. You are on a crazy . . . slope.
>
> For myself, I always come back to the King, to Jesus, to the Christian notion that all our efforts to make ourselves happy will fail, but that sacrifice for others will never fail. . . .
>
> As far as I am concerned, it is Christ or nothing. Goodbye and God bless you.

With that, Malcolm Muggeridge walked off the stage. And the students filed out with those words of judgment ringing in their ears (*Homiletics,* Oct./Dec. 1993).

Greed won't work; selfishness won't work; hostility won't work; materialism won't work; hedonism won't work; apathy won't work. The key to life is found in Jesus and his sacrificial love. If ever all of us could understand and embrace and commit ourselves to that, we could, with the help of God and by the grace of God, turn not only our nation but also our world right side up!

When you're a Christian, the whole world is from Missouri, saying, "Show me your vision."

Chapter 13

CAN THE WORLD SEE YOUR SERVANT SPIRIT?

As Jesus passed along the Sea of Galilee, he saw Simon and his brother Andrew casting a net into the sea—for they were fishermen. And Jesus said to them, "Follow me and I will make you fish for people." And immediately they left their nets and followed him. As he went a little farther, he saw James son of Zebedee and his brother John, who were in their boat mending the nets. Immediately he called them; and they left their father Zebedee in the boat with the hired men, and followed him.

—MARK 1:16-20

When I was a senior in high school, I was the quarterback on the football team. The Memphis Tech High Yellow Jackets—that's what we were called. Our best offensive play was the 46 Option pass or run. On this play, I would receive the ball from the center, take two quick steps to the right, fake the ball to the fullback, who would go off tackle, and as the defense converged on him, I would slide behind him and have the option to either pass or run. If the cornerback stayed back with our receiver, I would run; if he came up toward me, the receiver would be open, and I could pass the ball to him.

That was our "bread and butter" play, and it served us well—until one Friday night. That night, for some reason, the play simply would not work.

On the sidelines, the coaches said, "Jim, the key is the fake. If they don't take the fake to the fullback, the play doesn't have a chance." I couldn't figure out what was wrong. We were doing it just as we had always done it. The only difference was that our senior fullback, Gordon, had been injured and was not able to play that night.

His replacement was a tenth-grader named Mike. Mike had never played in a high school football game before, but he had great potential. He was big and fast and strong. But for some reason, when Mike was in the game, the 46 Option play would not work. We found out why the next morning!

We played our games on Friday nights, and on the following Saturday mornings, we watched a film of the games in slow motion, while the coaches pointed out our mistakes and applauded our good plays. As we watched the film that Saturday morning, we discovered dramatically why the 46 Option did not work the night before. You see, Mike was scared, and when I faked the handoff to him, he would run into the line with both hands held up high over his head, showing the opposing team that he didn't have the ball. He didn't want to be tackled, so he didn't carry through with the fake. He was not willing to sacrifice! He was not willing to lay himself on the line for the team, and that hurt the team. His unwillingness to do his part wrecked the play.

As I watched that truth unfold on the screen that Saturday morning, I realized how frightened Mike was and remembered that on two occasions the night before, when he was supposed to run the ball, he had run the wrong way from the handoff and acted as if he had gotten mixed up. Once he had run the right way, but refused to take the ball as I tried to hand it to him. He was so scared that he refused to try!

Now, the coaches—how shall I say this?—had a little visit with Mike behind closed doors! You'll be glad to know that they worked with him and helped him to overcome his fear, and he went on to become a very fine high school athlete.

Thinking of that experience recently, I realized that, sadly, there are lots of church members like Mike. They go through life with both hands held up high over their heads, saying in effect, "I want to be on the team, but I don't want to sacrifice that much. Let somebody else run the ball." They want to be Christians, but not servant Christians. But you see how mistaken that is. Service is what it's all about!

In Mark 1, when Jesus calls the disciples, he calls them to service. "Simon, Andrew, James, John—come, follow me. I have a job for you. I need your help. I want to put you to work. Come, join me in this ministry, and I will make you become fishers of people. Come, serve with me. Come, lay your life on the line with me. Come, sacrifice with me!" Being "servant Christians"—that's the ticket! If you want to please God, if you want to make the heart of God happy, if you want to do the will of God, if you want to feel a sense of meaning and purpose and fulfillment in your life, then take the ball and run with it. Become a servant Christian!

If you ever wonder about the significance of this call to servanthood, just remember this: No religion in the history of the world has ever emphasized service as Christianity does. You know why, don't you? Because our Lord was the humble, self-giving, suffering servant who sacrificed himself for us, who laid his life on the line for us, who at Calvary went "out on the limb" for us. Without question, we are called to be servant Christians.

Let me ask you something. How are you doing? Are you responding to the call? Are you running with the ball? Are you sacrificing yourself? Giving yourself? Offering yourself and your talents? Can you honestly say right now that you are a servant Christian?

As we think more about this together, let me outline three very special characteristics that are always present in the life of a servant Christian.

A Servant Christian Is Committed to Serving God

We, as Christian people, are called not to be dignitaries, not to be royalty, not to be aristocrats, but to be servants—God's servant people! It's so important to remember that, because the great temptation that always haunts and threatens us is to think of ourselves as privileged people, rather than as servant people; to think of ourselves as God's special favorites, rather than as God's humble servants. And when we give in to that temptation and begin to think of ourselves, and our rights, and our high place, and our benefits, and our special consideration, and our privileges—at that point, we depart from the spirit of Christ and fail to be God's church. As Christian disciples, we are not called for privilege, but for service; not to sit in high places, but to do hard work. We are not called because we are good, but because God is good. We are not called to have the red carpet rolled out to us, but to roll up our sleeves and get busy with God's work of redeeming this broken world.

If every member of the church understood that we are called to be servants—not privileged people, not "holier than thou" people—and embraced and practiced that, we could turn this world upside down for God. If every member of the church saw herself or himself as God's committed humble servant, 90 percent of our problems would be solved. We would have no staffing problems, no money problems, no burnout or dropout problems. No one would ever be offended or have their feelings hurt. No one would ever be difficult or resentful or jealous or petty or selfish. The servant mind-set is so important!

Some years ago, Dr. E. Stanley Jones founded a Christian community in India. He called it the Ashram. Converts would come there to live together to learn the Christian faith. One convert who came to the Ashram was a Brahman. You remember that the Brahmans were the upper class, the upper caste, the upper crust of society. Now, in this Christian Ashram, everyone present was expected to help with the community chores—mop the floors, wash the dishes, serve the meals, and even clean the bathhouses.

The former Brahman came to E. Stanley Jones and announced that he could not possibly perform such menial chores. They were beneath him, he said. But E. Stanley Jones told him that in Christ, there are no menial tasks, that all good works are sacred, and he should have no trouble as a Christian in mopping floors, washing dishes, or even cleaning bathhouses.

When the Brahman heard that, he said, "Brother Stanley, I'm converted—but not that far!"

Could that be our problem? We're converted, but not that far. Put that over against the servant spirit of Mother Teresa! She has a fascinating approach; she pretends that every single person she meets is Christ himself in disguise. She serves every person as if that person were Christ! This approach, of course, flows out of the words of Jesus in Matthew 25:40: "As you did it to one of the least of these . . . you did it to me."

When we have that kind of servant mind-set, no job is menial, and no task is beneath us, because in everything we do we are serving Christ, and that makes it sacred. A servant Christian is one who is committed to serving God.

A Servant Christian Is Responsive to the Needs of Others

His name is Father Mike. He is a Catholic priest in the Houston area and a friend of mine. In addition to being a priest, he is also a shade-tree mechanic. He loves to tinker with cars. Last summer, he was working on his car out in the church parking lot one afternoon. He had taken the carburetor apart, put it back together, and had the engine purring smoothly. When he finished, he had engine grease all over his hands. As he walked back toward his office in the church where he could clean up, he was holding his hands way out in front of him so he wouldn't get grease on his clothes.

As he approached the church playground, there was a five-year-old boy playing in the sandbox. The little boy saw Father Mike walking down the sidewalk with his hands extended. Immediately, the little boy left the sandbox, ran to Father Mike, and hugged him tightly around his legs. Then he ran back to play again in the sandbox.

Father Mike said, "What a beautiful moment that was! When that little boy saw me walking with my arms out like that, he thought I was looking for a hug! He thought I needed a hug! And he stopped what he was doing and ran to give me what he thought I needed."

Let me tell you something. There are a lot of people out there in the world today looking for a hug, needing a hug, starving for the embrace we can give them. That little boy had the Spirit of Christ in him that afternoon. He saw a need and rose to the occasion. How Christlike that is!

Christ did things like that all the time. He saw the need, responded with compassion, and reached out with help-ful, sacrificial love. The question for us to think about right now is this: Can we respond like that? Do we? Can we rise to the occasion like that? Can we reach out and give people the loving hugs they need? Can we serve like that? A servant Christian is responsive to the needs of others.

A Servant Christian Is Willing to Pay the Price

Once while I was giving a lecture series in Oklahoma, a powerful and prosperous oilman in the congregation invited me to go out to dinner with him and his family. Let me tell you about this oilman. He had been highly successful. He started out on the pipeline and over the years rose to the top. He had worked hard and done amazingly well. He was a self-made man. He had no formal education and consequently was a little rough around the edges, but he was very influential and wealthy.

We went to an elegant French restaurant which had beautiful fresh flowers everywhere, exquisite tablecloths, the finest china, silver, and crystal, and a very expensive menu.

When the waiter came over, the oilman said to me, "Now, Jim, you are our guest tonight. This is all on me. So you get anything you want—no, wait a minute. Let me have that menu. I'm going to order for you. I come in here all the time, and I know what's good."

Then, turning to the waiter, he said, "Bring him that 'Fee-let Mig-non.' " I couldn't help smiling at his mispronunciation of that entrée. But then it dawned on me: He may not be able to pronounce it, but he certainly can pay for it!

You and I can pronounce the word *service.* It rolls easily off the tongue. We can pronounce the phrase "servant Christian." But the question is: Can we pay for it? Can we pay the price? A servant Christian is committed to serving God, is responsive to the needs of others, and is willing and able to pay the price.

The choice is ours. Will we throw up our hands? Or will we take the ball and run with it?

When you're a Christian, the whole world is from Missouri, saying, "Show me your servant spirit."

Chapter 14

CAN THE WORLD SEE YOUR COMPASSION?

*N*ow *when Jesus returned, the crowd welcomed him, for they were all waiting for him. Just then there came a man named Jairus, a leader of the synagogue. He fell at Jesus' feet and begged him to come to his house, for he had an only daughter, about twelve years old, who was dying. As he went, the crowds pressed in on him. Now there was a woman who had been suffering from hemorrhages for twelve years; and though she had spent all she had on physicians, no one could cure her. She came up behind him and touched the fringe of his clothes, and immediately her hemorrhage stopped. Then Jesus asked, "Who touched me?" When all denied it, Peter said, "Master, the crowds surround you and press in on you." But Jesus said, "Someone touched me; for I noticed that power had gone out from me." When the woman saw that she could not remain hidden, she came trembling; and falling down before him, she declared in the presence of all the people why she had touched him, and how she had been immediately healed. He said to her, "Daughter, your faith has made you well; go in peace."*

—LUKE 8:40-48

Dr. John Henry Jowett, a great British preacher of a generation ago, told the story of a young servant girl who had no formal education, yet was deeply spiritual. She had a strong sense of compassion, a concern for people.

When Dr. Jowett visited with her one day and asked how she spent her days, she said, "My work is very demanding, and I don't get much time off, so I can't serve the church as much as I would like. But I have come up with a plan that lets me do what I can."

"What is that?" asked Dr. Jowett.

She replied, "Well, I always take the daily paper to bed with me at night."

Dr. Jowett was puzzled. "Tell me about that. I don't understand."

"Well," she said, "I read the page with the birth notices, and I pray for the babies that have been born; then I read the marriages, and I pray that they may be happy and true; and next I read the deaths, and I pray that God's comfort may come to those sorrowing homes" (Robert E. Luccock, *The Power of His Name* [Harper & Brothers, 1960]).

That young girl was not far from the Kingdom. Why? Because she had discovered the spirit of loving compassion.

Loving compassion—Jesus called it the most significant sign of discipleship. In John's Gospel, he said it like this: "I give you a new commandment, that you love one another. Just as I have loved you, you also should love one another. By this everyone will know that you are my disciples" (John 13:34-35). Jesus not only taught compassion, he lived it. As deftly and as quickly as a magnetic needle points to the north, so the heart of Jesus immediately zeroed in on the neediest person in the crowd.

How quickly Jesus noticed a rejected and lonely Zacchaeus up in that sycamore tree. How swiftly he sensed the intensity and urgency in the cry of blind Bartimaeus on the roadside. In each case, he reached out with compassion to give the help that was needed. We see it again in this tender story in Luke 8.

Jesus is on his way to see a little girl who is critically ill, when suddenly he is interrupted. As he is moving through a large enthusiastic crowd, a woman who has been hemorrhaging nonstop for twelve years discreetly slips up behind Jesus and timidly touches the hem of his robe. The story tells us that right then, her bleeding stops. She thinks she has gone unnoticed, so she drops back, trying to lose herself in the huge crowd. But Jesus turns around and asks, "Who touched me?"

The disciples are astonished and somewhat put out by Jesus' question. "Who touched you? What do you mean, who touched you? The crowd is pressing in all around us, pushing and shoving. Everybody is touching everybody. What kind of question is that?" But Jesus knows that it was a special touch. How perceptive he was!

He begins to look around. The woman had not expected to be found out. But now she fearfully steps forward and tells Jesus that she has been bleeding for so long—more than twelve years—and that she has tried everything— doctors, medicines, magic, wives' tales, and supersti- tions—to no avail, no improvement. In fact, she has only become worse. She tells Jesus that she has heard about him and his power to heal, and she believed that if she could just touch his clothing, she could be made well. And it worked! The bleeding has stopped!

Jesus' heart goes out to her, and he speaks to her tenderly: "Daughter, your faith has made you well; go in peace."

In this fascinating story, we not only see the compas- sionate spirit of Jesus, but we also discover some of the key characteristics of compassion—special qualities that we, as followers of Jesus, need to cultivate in our lives. Let's take a look at some of these.

Compassion Is Sensitive to the Needs of Others

Compassion is aware, tuned in, responsive, sensitive to the needs of others. Hundreds of people were pressing in upon Jesus that day in that crowded and busy street.

Picture it in your mind. They were thronging around him, pushing and shoving and clamoring, reaching out to him. Yet out of that mass of humanity, Jesus became aware of one person, one need, one touch. He felt something unique and special as that woman tried to secretly touch the hem of his robe. How sensitive he was!

To bring this closer to home, let me tell you a true story. It happened on Father's Day some years ago. I had preached in the 8:45 A.M. service that morning, and then rushed to teach Sunday school. After Sunday school, I charged frantically back to my office to quickly skim over my sermon notes and get ready for the 11:00 service, which now was only minutes away.

However, when I arrived at my office, there was absolute pandemonium. People were waiting for me. Someone wanted to tell me about a friend who had been taken to the hospital. Some former members who had moved away were back home and wanted to speak to me. A young couple I had married two weekends before had just returned from their honeymoon and stopped by to say "Hi." Three staff members were there to remind me of special announcements that needed to be made in the upcoming service. An usher was there with a note about a car in the parking lot with its lights on, doors locked, and motor running. Another staff member was there to introduce me to some visitors who were prospective members. Still another was there to tell me that one of the babies scheduled to be baptized in the next service had not shown up yet.

It was now four minutes before the service was to begin, and the clock was ticking relentlessly. As I was trying to deal with all these things, at the same time grab my Bible and hymnal and sermon notes and put on my robe, suddenly I felt a persistent tug at the back of my robe. I turned around. It was our daughter, Jodi. She was eight years old at the time. She had worked her way through the crowd and was tugging on my robe, insistently motioning for me to bend down. She had something to tell me.

My first response was—how shall I say this?—parental! I thought, "Jodi, couldn't this wait until we get in the car after church? I'm doing big stuff up here!" But I didn't say that. There was something about that tug, and God was with me, giving me the good sense to realize it. So I shut everything else out and dropped down on one knee to be on eye level with Jodi.

She beamed as she said, "Daddy, it's Father's Day, and I have a special present for you. I made it in Sunday school this morning, and I want to give it to you right now because I love you so much, and I'm so glad that you are my daddy!" She handed me the present.

It was a Father's Day card she had made with construction paper and crayons. On the front cover was a picture of the earth as seen from a spaceship, with these words: "To the Bestest Father in the whole wide world." On page two was a Polaroid picture of Jodi making the card in Sunday school class. It had been taken by her teacher. On page three were the words, "Happy Birthday," marked through and followed by the words "Oops! I mean— Happy Father's Day." Beneath that was this note: "Everybody makes mistakes." The back cover had three more words: "I Love You."

After I read the card out loud, Jodi's face lit up with a proud smile. She wrapped her arms around my neck, hugged me tightly, and whispered in my ear, "Dad, I love you even when it's not Father's Day." I hugged her back, and in that moment we became the whole world for each other. In that moment, "time stood still."

Think what I would have missed if I had said to her, "Not now, Jodi! I'm too busy!" Think what that would have done to her spirit.

I was a few minutes late for church that day, but it didn't matter, because somewhere in heaven, God was smiling!

Jesus had so many great moments like that with people, and sadly, the truth is, we have so few. Jesus had so many tender moments when time stood still. He could feel the touch, hear the cry, sense the need, zero in on the person, seize the moment. You know why, don't you? Because he was compassionate, and being compassionate means, first of all, being sensitive to the needs of others. Over and over in the Gospels, Jesus shows us how to tune in to the needs of people, how to be aware, how to be sensitive.

Compassion Takes Advantage of Interruptions

I skimmed through the Gospels and put together what I consider a very impressive list of stories. Read the list and see if you can find the common thread:

The Parable of the Good Samaritan
The Greatest Commandment
The Blessing of the Little Children
The Healing of the Gerasene Demoniac
The Healing of the Ten Lepers
The Healing of the Paralytic
The Healing of the man who was blind from birth
The Rich Young Ruler encounter
Zacchaeus
Blind Bartimaeus
Nicodemus
The Cross . . . and the Resurrection

What do these stories have in common? They are all special moments in the Scriptures, and all were produced by interruptions! Jesus, with his compassionate heart, took advantage of those interruptions, redeemed them, and used them to do good. We see it again here in Luke 8. Jesus was on his way to see the critically ill daughter of Jairus when he healed the woman of her hemorrhage.

This raises a poignant question that should haunt all of us: How many special moments have we missed? How many special moments with our children, our mates, our friends, our coworkers, or even strangers, have we missed because we were too tired, too busy, or too preoccupied? In addition to being sensitive to the needs of others, compassion takes advantage of interruptions.

Compassion Is Gracious

Notice how gracious Jesus is to the hemorrhaging woman. He calls her "daughter," an obvious term of endearment. He doesn't fuss at her or criticize her or question her. He doesn't condemn her for being superstitious. He doesn't even give her a theology lesson. He just meets her where she is. He accepts her, encourages her, and heals her in a gracious way. He doesn't take the credit for the healing. Instead, he gives her faith the credit: "Your faith has made you well!" How gracious he was!

I have been in the ministry for more than thirty years, and over the years I have noticed something very significant. The great Christians all possess this magnificent spirit of graciousness and humility.

Once while on a speaking engagement in another state, I attended a dinner party. The host was bragging loudly about how he had been active in a great church in that city for thirty-seven years, and how close he was to a series of truly outstanding ministers who had served that church during that span of time. But when a certain man's name was mentioned, the host became livid. I cringed inside as he let loose with a harsh, hostile tirade against the named man. His criticism was cruel, unfair, vindictive, and sprinkled with expletives. He finished by saying, "I'll never speak to him again as long as I live!"

I found myself wondering, What has he been hearing in church all these years? How could he go to church regularly for thirty-seven years and hear the gospel preached by those outstanding ministers Sunday after Sunday, and still know nothing of graciousness, compassion, or forgiveness? How can we be exposed to the life and teachings and spirit of Jesus and not realize the importance of love, mercy, and grace? Our Lord's bigness of spirit, our Lord's love, is a constant call and challenge to us to be compassionate, gracious people. Compassion is sensitive; it takes advantage of interruptions; it is gracious.

Compassion Is Active

It's not enough to just feel compassion. We must do something about it. Compassion can't sit still. Jesus shows us that again and again. Compassion is love at work. It is active! Remember how the poet put it:

> Love in your heart isn't put there to stay;
> Love isn't love 'til you give it away.

When you're a Christian, the whole world is from Missouri, saying, "Show me your compassion."

Chapter 15

CAN THE WORLD SEE YOUR PERSEVERANCE?

F or it is as if a man, going on a journey, summoned his slaves and entrusted his property to them; to one he gave five talents, to another two, to another one, to each according to his ability. Then he went away. The one who had received the five talents went off at once and traded with them, and made five more talents. In the same way, the one who had the two talents made two more talents. But the one who had received the one talent went off and dug a hole in the ground and hid his master's money. After a long time the master of those slaves came and settled accounts with them. Then the one who had received the five talents came forward, bringing five more talents, saying, 'Master, you handed over to me five talents; see, I have made five more talents.' His master said to him, 'Well done, good and trustworthy slave; you have been trustworthy in a few things, I will put you in charge of many things; enter into the joy of your master.' And the one with the two talents also came forward, saying, 'Master, you handed over to me two talents; see, I have made two more talents.' His master said to him, 'Well done, good and trustworthy slave; you have been trustworthy in a few things, I will put you in charge of many things; enter into the joy of your master.' Then the one who had received the one talent also came forward, saying, 'Master, I knew that you were a harsh man, reaping where you did not sow, and gathering where you did not scatter seed; so I was afraid, and I went and hid your talent in the ground. Here you have what is yours.' But his master replied, 'You wicked and lazy slave! You *knew, did you, that I reap where I did not sow, and gather where I did not scatter? Then you ought to have invested my money with the bankers, and on my return I would have received what was my own with interest. So take the talent from him, and give it to the one with the ten talents. For to all those who have, more will be given, and they will have an abundance; but from those who have nothing, even what they have will be taken away."*

—MATTHEW 25:14-29

A friend once shared with me a fascinating article from the *Fort Worth Star-Telegram,* written by a man named Dave Ferman (April 5, 1994). In it Ferman graphically described a disturbing trend that has been running rampant across our nation in recent times. The article was titled, "It's Not My Fault: For Every Misdeed It Seems There Was a Lousy Childhood":

> Listen carefully, and you'll hear Americans passing the buck—over and over again. It's a short sentence, but one that's been at the heart of the American psyche. You'll hear it in courtrooms and every afternoon on "Oprah," you'll hear it all over the halls of academia and flitting across Capitol Hill. You'll know it. You've said it. But we'll remind you: "Don't Blame me—It's Not My Fault!"
>
> No matter what, no matter how far we have to stretch, we find someone else to blame for our problems and our misdeeds. Whether it's our lousy childhoods, or our lack of dates in high school, or heavy metal music or alcohol or drugs—well, it's not our fault! If we beat our kid, or did all that cocaine, or shot that police officer, or turned our lives into a big, ugly mess—it's not really our fault. Nope, not us. No way.

Ferman goes on to describe the most celebrated examples of our time, such as the Menendez Brothers, Tonya Harding, Ted Bundy. They, and many others, admitted their misdeeds, but then quickly explained them away by saying things such as, "A poor childhood made me do it";

"abuse made me do it"; "TV violence made me do it"; "pornography made me do it"; "peer pressure made me do it"; "mob madness made me do it."

Ferman recalled the case in Texas when a young man shot a DPS trooper point-blank on a lonely stretch of highway, and later said, "I'm not really to blame! Rap music made me do it!" Then Dave Ferman made this poignant statement: "If the '80's were the Me Decade, the '90's have become the 'Hey Not Me Decade'—an era when blaming anyone else for mistakes and misdeeds has become an accepted cultural standard."

The point is clear: We are living in very frank times when people will openly admit to almost anything, but then just as quick justify everything by pointing the accusing finger at someone or something else. In essence, they say, "Yes, Lord, I have sinned, but it's not really my fault!" This technique of blame shifting is permeating our society in a frighteningly accelerated way these days, but actually, the ploy is as old as the Bible.

We see something of this in the parable of the talents. A more contemporary name might be the "parable of the investments." Like all of Jesus' parables, it is simple, yet so profound in its message.

A well-to-do businessman decided to take a trip. The man had three associates with whom he left his fortune. To these three men, he parceled out his holdings. To one, he gave $50,000 in silver. To another, he gave $20,000 in silver. And to still another, he gave $10,000. He instructed the men to work with the money, to use the money, to invest the money for an appropriate return and profit.

Some time later, when the businessman returned home from his travels, he called in his three associates for a report. The first two men had invested their money wisely and carefully, and had done quite well. They were commended for a job well done. But the third man did not fare so well. He had been afraid—afraid even to try. So he had done nothing but hide the money. His lack of imagination, courage, and effort cost his boss dearly—and ultimately it cost him his job.

But let's go back a minute. Look at what the third man said as he came in to give his report. The very first words out of his mouth were: "Master, I knew you to be a hard man, so I was afraid, and I went and hid your money in the ground. Here, take back what is yours." In other words, he was saying, "I didn't work. I didn't try. I didn't even make an effort. But it's not really my fault. Actually, Master, it's really your fault, because I knew you had high expectations, and that scared me, paralyzed me, froze me up. You're the guilty one, because you put all that fear in me. So I'm not really responsible. Yes, Master, I failed, but it's not really my fault."

These are the words of a man who has quit on life and now spends his days pointing the accusing finger of blame at everybody else. Psychologists tell us that as long as we live, we have two desires working within us, doing battle against one another. One is the desire to give up, to pull back, to throw in the towel and quit on life. The other is the desire to move forward through struggle and effort, risking and stretching and growing and striving and celebrating life.

Of course, the call of the Christian is to move forward and embrace life. But sadly, far too many people are like the third man in the parable—the one-talent servant. They give up and give in to the desire to quit on life. They start out well, with starry eyes and great fervor, ready to conquer the world and live life to the full; but then along come the pressures, the problems, the difficulties, the challenges, the responsibilities, the burdens, the disappointments, the heartaches, and the stresses. Suddenly, they feel hoodwinked and deceived. They feel persecuted and put upon. They feel cheated. They feel that life has dealt them a poor hand—a hand not nearly as favorable as others are holding. They get only one talent, while others get ten. For a while, they scream, "Unfair!" Then they quietly fold up their tents and give up. No longer do they really live. They pull back into a hard shell. Life for them becomes merely a series of escapes. They vegetate; they exist; they get by; they use most of their energy blaming somebody else for their problems; they walk around and seem to be alive, but in essence, they have quit on life.

Please don't let that happen to you. Don't give up on life. Let me be more specific by underscoring three important things we must never give up on in life.

Don't Give Up on Goodness

My good friend Grady Earls placed on my desk a thoughtful article that had been written by a man named Dr. Pat Prouty. Grady had scribbled across the top of the article these words: "Fodder for Preaching." Grady was right. Dr. Pat Prouty, who is a past president of the Texas Veterinary Medicine Association, wrote this article about ethics and goodness in today's world. Here's part of what he had to say:

> Normally, I sleep like a baby. I fell asleep one time in the middle of the gulf, in the middle of a storm, in the middle of the night—all by myself in my sailboat. My wife sometimes thinks I am crazy. One time I fell asleep while riding on an elephant in the jungles of Southern India. This story is not about a peaceful snooze however. It's about a restless dream-filled night I recently had—in my own bed.
>
> I dreamed that our society was falling apart at the seams. I dreamed our teenagers were armed with automatic weapons. I dreamed that muggings and rape and even murder were becoming commonplace. I dreamed that the police seemed helpless against an ever-increasing epidemic of vandalism. I even dreamed that our professions were caught up in an ever-increasing attitude of competi-

tiveness. Members of our legal profession were being held up in ridicule. Things were so bad that our governing leaders felt that if something weren't done soon, our civilization would self-destruct.

The President came up with a magnificent plan. They would build a giant supercomputer, bigger and smarter than anything ever conceived before. When it was completed, they entered all the knowledge that humankind had accumulated since the beginning of time. It took large teams of scientists months to collect and enter the data. When they were done, the President asked the computer to answer one question: "What laws can we pass that will save society?"

Once the question was entered, lights started flashing, bells started ringing, buzzers started buzzing, and after several minutes, the printer started printing. The single page report was sent to the President. The President appeared that night on "Larry King Live," and read the following:

"In order to save society, we must obey the following laws:

1. You shall have no other gods but the one true God.
2. You shall not make for yourself a graven image.
3. You shall not take the name of God in vain.
4. You shall remember the Sabbath and keep it holy.
5. You shall honor your father and mother.
6. You shall not kill.
7. You shall not commit adultery.
8. You shall not steal.
9. You shall not bear false witness.
10. You shall not covet anything that belongs to a neighbor."

Dr. Prouty concluded his article with these words: "I woke up then with a great sense of relief. Now we know what to do. I guess we knew it all along. All we have to do is believe in it."

If the third man in the parable of the talents had done what his master had commanded—if he had done faithfully what his master told him to do—he would have come out all right. But he didn't! He didn't trust the system. He didn't even try. He had long ago given up on life and on goodness.

Don't Give Up on Graciousness

When will we ever learn? The third man in the parable tried to put the blame on someone else, and his unkindness came back to haunt him.

There is a story about a man in a large city who was on his way to an interview for a new job with a highly successful company. Well-groomed, wearing a nice suit and smelling of expensive cologne, the man made his way to the corporate headquarters. As he was waiting for the elevator, an elderly janitor walked by, slipped on the wet floor, and fell down awkwardly. The young man chuckled to himself at the Three-Stooges-like humor, unconcerned that the older man might have been hurt. He actually stepped over the fallen janitor, boarded the elevator, went up to the twenty-ninth floor, and entered the reception area of the firm.

Soon his name was called, and he was ushered into a beautiful executive office. He was greeted by the woman who was going to conduct the interview. She was the company president. Immediately, she said, "By the way, on your way up to see me, did you see anyone who needed help?"

"Yes," he replied, "an elderly janitor fell down right in front of me as I was waiting for the elevator."

"Did you stop to help him?" she asked.

"Well, no, because I believe in promptness, and I didn't want to be late for this very important interview."

"Of course," said the company president, "but you see, that was the interview! As a business executive, I know that many people do try to push and shove their way to the top. But as a Christian, I have come to realize that love is the most powerful thing in the world, and anyone who wishes to rank first must remain the last and the servant of all. I'm very sorry, but I'm afraid you are not the kind of person I have in mind for this position."

As Jesus made his way to the cross, the disciples were arguing over who was the greatest among them. When they entered the upper room, they were still arrogantly arguing and complaining. There Jesus took a towel and basin and he washed their feet, showing them and us in a dramatic way that we are called as Christians to be gracious servants. Please don't give up on goodness, and please don't give up on graciousness.

Don't Give Up on God

A woman who had taught Sunday school for many years received an unexpected letter one day from a young man in the hospital.

"You probably don't remember me," he wrote, "but I visited your Sunday school class when I was staying with my grandparents during the summer of 1978. You were kind to me. Because of you, I became a Christian, and my faith has been so very important to me, especially now that I have been diagnosed with cancer. So I just wanted to write and tell you 'thanks.' "

She didn't remember the young man at all, but when she searched through her 1978 diary, she came across this notation: "We had a visitor in class today. He was a handful! Couldn't sit still. I sat beside him and gave him some extra attention. Don't know whether I did him any good or not" (Kent Melcher, *Word & Witness* 7/11/93).

As Christians, it is not our task to worry about success. Our calling is to be faithful, to sow the seed, to live our faith every day, to do the best we can, and to trust God to bring the harvest—trust God to bring it out right.

The point is clear. We don't need a scapegoat because we have a Savior, so don't quit on life! Seize life! Taste life! Celebrate life!

When you're a Christian, the whole world is from Missouri, saying, "Show me your perseverance." In other words, show me your faith; show me your hope; show me your love. So come what may, hang in there! Trust in God and live your faith daily. Don't give up on goodness. Don't give up on graciousness. And whatever you do, don't give up on God!

SUGGESTIONS FOR LEADING A STUDY OF WHEN YOU'RE A CHRISTIAN, THE WHOLE WORLD IS FROM MISSOURI

This book by James W. Moore offers many practical ideas for living a life of faith in a "show me" world. As a discussion leader, you have the opportunity to help the members of your group become more effective Christians. Here are some suggestions to keep in mind as you begin:

1. You should read the entire book before your first group meeting so you have an overview of the book and can be a better guide for the members of your group. You may want to use a highlighter to designate important points.

2. Hand out the book to participants before the first session and ask them to read the first chapter before your initial meeting. You may want to limit the size of your group to less than ten members so everyone gets a chance to participate.

3. Begin each session by reviewing the main points using the chapter summary. You may ask group members what they saw as highlights. Use your leader's guide to suggest other main points.

4. Select the discussion questions and activities in advance. Use the ones you think will work best. You may want to ask the questions in a different order from how they are listed in the leader's guide. Allow a set amount of time for questions and a set amount of time for one or two activities. Create your own questions or activities if you desire.

5. Before moving from questions to activities, ask members if they have any questions that have not been answered.

6. Following the conclusion of the activity, close with a short prayer. If your group desires, pause for individual prayer petitions.

7. Start your meetings on time and end them on schedule.
8. If you ask a question and no one volunteers an answer, begin the discussion by suggesting an answer yourself. Then ask for comments and other answers.
9. Encourage total participation by asking questions of specific members. Your role is to give everyone who wants a chance to talk. Remember, you can always ask the question "Why?" to continue a discussion.
10. Be thankful and supportive. Thank members for their ideas and participation.

Chapter 1

Can the World See Your Christian Gumption?

Chapter Summary

1. By living your faith, the world can see your Christian gumption.
2. To have Christian gumption means to live life unselfishly.
3. To have Christian gumption means to love people unconditionally.
4. To have Christian gumption means to trust God unreservedly.

Discussion Questions

1. What new insights did you receive from reading this chapter?
2. Did you see the movie *Forrest Gump*? If so, what impressed you about it?
3. Why is a summary of Gump's life a good synopsis of the teachings of Jesus in the Sermon on the Mount?
4. Recall an unselfish act someone once did for you. How did it make you feel?
5. How does it feel to perform an unselfish act?
6. What does it mean to love unconditionally?
7. Tell about who has loved you or whom you have loved unconditionally.
8. What does it mean to trust God unreservedly?
9. List people you trust and say why you trust them.
10. What motivates us to trust or love someone unconditionally?
11. Why can't we escape God's love?
12. What "Gumption" does the Sermon on the Mount contain?

Practical Applications/Activities

1. Go out of your way this week to do an unselfish act. Report back to the group.
2. Give someone unconditional love this week. Report back to the group.
3. Make a commitment to trust God with one issue in your life.
4. Discuss: What prevents us from trusting God without reservation?
5. Brainstorm specific ideas for living life unselfishly.

Prayer: *Dear God, we thank you for your unconditional love. Help us to love others as you love us and commit unselfish acts each day. Be with us during this coming week. Amen.*

Chapter 2

Can the World See Your Spirit of Forgiveness?

Chapter Summary

1. By living your faith the world can see your spirit of forgiveness.
2. We need to recognize our own need for forgiveness.
3. We need to accept God's gracious forgiveness.
4. We need to pass forgiveness on to others.

Discussion Questions

1. What new insights did you receive from reading this chapter?
2. In your own words, explain what it means to have a spirit of forgiveness.
3. What makes it so hard to forgive at times?

4. What is the cost of forgiveness, the price we pay when we forgive?
5. What benefits do we receive when we forgive someone? What benefits does the forgiven person receive?
6. Tell about a time you were forgiven by someone. How did you feel?
7. Tell about a time you forgave someone. How did you feel?
8. What happens to us when we don't forgive?
9. Why would someone not accept forgiveness? Does everyone want forgiveness?
10. Explain: We live daily in the spirit of forgiveness.
11. Read Matthew 18:21-33 again. What impressed you about the story of the king and the two slaves?
12. What can we do when we don't have the strength to forgive someone?

Practical Applications/Activities

1. Discuss incidents of forgiveness found in the Bible.
2. List ways the world can see Christian forgiveness in action.
3. Discuss the crime of murder in relation to forgiveness.
4. Write a note to someone you need to forgive.
5. Write a list of debts you owe to others.

Prayer: *Dear God, we thank you for the gift of forgiveness. Please forgive us as we forgive others. Help us to show the world our spirit of forgiveness and your love for us all. Amen.*

Chapter 3

Can the World See Your Dedication?

Chapter Summary

1. By living your faith the world can see your dedication.
2. We can dedicate a life of kindness to Christ.

3. We can dedicate a life of courage to Christ.
4. We can dedicate a life of service to Christ.

Discussion Questions

1. What new insights did you receive from reading this chapter?
2. In your own words, explain what dedication means to you.
3. Recall a time when you witnessed dedication in action.
4. What is the price we pay for being dedicated to a cause?
5. What are the benefits of being dedicated?
6. Is it ever wrong to be dedicated? In what way?
7. What are the roadblocks to dedication?
8. Discuss your thoughts concerning John 21:15-19.
9. Explain what it means to live a life of kindness.
10. Explain what it means to dedicate a life of courage to Christ.
11. Why does the world value dedication?
12. List examples of major accomplishments resulting from dedicated individuals.

Practical Applications/Activities

1. Discuss ways the world can see Christian dedication at work.
2. Write a dedication for your life's story or for a future book you would like to write.
3. Look at and discuss book dedications in your church library.
4. Dedicate yourself to one objective this coming week.
5. Select a book from your church library and read about a dedicated Christian.

Prayer: *Jesus, we thank you for your dedication and love for us. We praise you for all you have done for us and for* *others. Help us to be dedicated to you and be your hands and voice in this world. In your name; Amen.*

Chapter 4

Can the World See Your Resilience?

Chapter Summary

1. By living your faith, the world can see your resilience.
2. We can be resilient in our disappointments and heartaches.
3. We can be resilient in our service to God.
4. We can be resilient in our relations with people.

Discussion Questions

1. What new insights did you receive from reading this chapter?
2. In your own words, explain what resilience means.
3. Share a time when you were resilient. How did you feel?
4. How do we become resilient? How do we find the power to weather life's storms?
5. How does Mark 15:1-15 show the resilience of Jesus?
6. What is the opposite of resilience?
7. Name some storms of life that we all need resilience from.
8. Name some famous people known for their resilience.
9. How can we be resilient in our service to God?
10. How can we be resilient in our relations with others?
11. How does being resilient help us become better Christians?
12. What makes it so difficult to be resilient at times?

Practical Applications/Activities

1. Discuss some famous athletes who have been resilient.

2. Discuss the topic of resilience with your family or a friend this week.
3. Read an article about someone who is resilient.
4. Practice resilience in your life this week.
5. List ways you can encourage others to be resilient.

Prayer: *Dear God, thank you for making us a resilient people and able to overcome the obstacles in this world. Help us to remember we can always be resilient because you are with us. Be with us this week. Amen.*

Chapter 5

Can the World See Your Gratitude?

Chapter Summary

1. By living your faith, the world can see your gratitude.
2. Gratitude is the language of the Christian.
3. Gratitude is the fragrance of the Christian.
4. Gratitude is the lifestyle of the Christian.

Discussion Questions

1. What new insights did you receive from reading this chapter?
2. What is gratitude? Explain what it means to you.
3. Recall a time when you expressed gratitude.
4. Share an incident when someone expressed gratitude to you.
5. What are the benefits of gratitude?
6. What prevents some people from having a spirit of gratitude?
7. Why can we have gratitude to God in all circumstances?
8. How can gratitude be a fragrance of a Christian?

9. Explain: Gratitude is the language of the Christian.
10. What are the keys to unconditional gratitude?
11. Explain how gratitude can be a Christian lifestyle.
12. How does a spirit of gratitude make us better Christians?

Practical Applications/Activities

1. Discuss examples of gratitude found in the Bible.
2. List ways we can express gratitude to God and others.
3. Discuss strategies for enhancing our spirit of gratitude.
4. Make a list of things and people you are grateful for.
5. Practice gratitude this week.

Prayer: *Jesus, we are grateful for your love and so many things in our lives. Help us to remember that you are the giver of life and all good things. May we be thankful to you at all times and in all circumstances. Amen.*

Chapter 6

Can the World See Your Faith?

Chapter Summary

1. We need the world to see our faith through word and deed.
2. The cross is a symbol of faith.
3. The cross is a symbol of love.
4. The cross is a symbol of hope.

Discussion Questions

1. What new insights did you receive from reading this chapter?
2. How does faith give us a new perspective on life?
3. Talk about what having faith means to you.

4. Why is the cross the center of our faith?
5. How is the cross a symbol of our faith?
6. What does the cross remind us of?
7. How is the cross a symbol of hope?
8. How is the cross a symbol of love?
9. How are faith, hope, and love related?
10. Where does faith come from?
11. Recall a time when you acted on faith.
12. What are the benefits of having a strong faith?

Practical Applications/Activities

1. Discuss some strategies for living your faith.
2. Carry a small cross with you this week to remind you of your faith.
3. Talk about your faith with your family or with a friend.
4. Make a list of people of faith in the Bible.
5. Write your own faith creed.

Prayer: *Jesus, we thank you for the gift of faith. Forgive us for lacking faith at times. Help us to be bold in our faith and remember your faithfulness to us. Please be with us this week. Amen.*

Chapter 7

Can the World See
Your Christian Witness?

Chapter Summary

1. By living your faith the world can see your Christian witness.
2. Show your witness by the way you speak.
3. Show your witness by the way you treat others.

4. Show your witness by the way you serve the church.
5. Show your witness by the way you trust God.

Discussion Questions

1. What new insights did you receive from reading this chapter?
2. In your own words, explain what it means to be a Christian witness.
3. Who has been a Christian witness to you? In what ways?
4. Why do we need more Christian witnesses?
5. What does it mean to be a witness for God?
6. How do we get the power to witness?
7. List some keys to witnessing by the words we speak.
8. What words, written or spoken, have influenced your faith?
9. What actions toward others reflect our faith?
10. How can we be a Christian witness by the way we treat people?
11. How does your service to the church serve as a witness to your faith?
12. How are trusting God and witnessing related?

Practical Applications/Activities

1. Witness to someone by words or actions this week.
2. Invite someone to church next Sunday.
3. List different ways you can be a witness.
4. Thank someone for being a Christian witness to you.
5. Name one way you will be a better witness in the future.

Prayer: *Dear God, we are called to be your witnesses to others. Help us to be effective in sharing the good news of the gospel. Thank you for giving us all we need to be good witnesses. May we put our faith into action this week. Amen.*

Chapter 8

Can the World See Your Love?

Chapter Summary

1. By living your faith, the world can see your love.
2. We express our love with words.
3. We express our love with attitudes.
4. We express our love with actions.

Discussion Questions

1. What new insights did you receive from reading this chapter?
2. What are the risks of Christian love?
3. Tell about someone who showed you Christian love.
4. In your own words, tell what Christian love means to you.
5. What impressed you about the story of Jesus and the woman whose child had a demon?
6. Why do we have trouble speaking words of love to others?
7. What does it mean to "live by the attitude of love"?
8. How can others benefit from love in action?
9. Name some famous people who are examples of Christian love.
10. What motivates us to love others?
11. What stories in the Bible illustrate love in action?
12. How can prayer and reading the Bible express our love?

Practical Applications/Activities

1. List ways we can make love our attitude in life.
2. List ways we can show love through our actions.
3. Visit a nursing home or a shut-in this week.

4. List three ways you can be more effective in sharing God's love.
5. Focus on having a "love attitude" at work or at home this week.

Prayer: *Jesus, your love surrounds us. Help us to surround others with Christian love through our words, our attitudes and our actions. Thank you for your love and for always being near us. In your name; Amen.*

Chapter 9

Can the World See Your Bigness of Spirit?

Chapter Summary

1. By living your faith the world can see your bigness of spirit.
2. Life is too short for pettiness.
3. Life is too short for hurt feelings.
4. Life is too short for bitterness and ill will.

Discussion Questions

1. What new insights did you receive from reading this chapter?
2. What lessons can we learn from Luke 6:32-36?
3. What is bigness of spirit?
4. How are we hurt when we give in to toxic attitude?
5. Recall a past bitterness in your life and how it turned out later.
6. How can we focus on love and forgiveness?
7. When we are petty, whom do we cut off?
8. Who taught you about bigness of spirit as a child?
9. Who showed you bigness of spirit recently as an adult?

10. What is the cost of having bigness of spirit?
11. What are the benefits of having bigness of spirit?
12. What stories in the Bible illustrate bigness of spirit?

Practical Applications/Activities

1. Identify and attempt to mend a relationship hurt by bitterness.
2. Help someone achieve bigness of spirit.
3. Write a note of forgiveness to someone who has hurt you.
4. List ways that Christians can show bigness of spirit.
5. Perform an act of bigness of spirit this week.

Prayer: *Dear God, thank you for giving us the ability to forgive others. Help us not to be separated from others through pettiness, hurt feelings, bitterness and ill will. May we serve as your ambassadors of love and put our faith into action. Amen.*

Chapter 10

Can the World See Your Kinship to God?

Chapter Summary

1. By living your faith, the world can see your kinship to God.
2. By the way we love, people can see our kinship to God.
3. By the way we laugh, people can see our kinship to God.
4. By the way we live, people can see our kinship to God.

Discussion Questions

1. What new insights did you receive from reading this chapter?
2. What lessons do we learn from Mark 3:31-35?
3. What does having kinship to God mean to you?
4. What type of behavior shows kinship to God?

5. Recall an incident where you saw a kinship to God in someone.
6. What kind of commitment is needed for kinship?
7. What are the benefits of laughter?
8. What are the benefits of love?
9. Talk about someone you know who has a gift of laughter.
10. What responsibilities do we have as kin to God?
11. How do we become kin to God?
12. Talk about someone who showed their kinship through their love to you.

Practical Applications/Activities

1. Pay attention to your words and humor this week.
2. List some ways you can show people your Christian love.
3. Name some examples of famous people who showed their kinship.
4. Discuss examples in the Bible of people who showed kinship through their behavior.
5. List ten ways to live that show your faith.

Prayer: *Dear God, we thank you that you created us and sustain us. We are your children. Help us to act in ways that please you and accomplish your will. Give us strength and courage to live out our faith each day. Amen.*

Chapter 11

Can the World See Your Strength in Facing Stress?

Chapter Summary

1. By living your faith, you have the strength to face stress.
2. Bring your stress to God.

3. God can help you turn problems into opportunities.
4. Do something positive with stress in your life.

Discussion Questions

1. What new insights did you receive from reading this chapter?
2. What lessons do we learn from Matthew 11:25-30?
3. How do we get strength from God to fight stress?
4. Discuss what causes stress in your life.
5. Share how you try to relieve stress.
6. How can we elevate stress and use it to serve God?
7. Name a problem that you turned into an opportunity.
8. Name some situations in which stress can be a friend.
9. What is the relationship between stress and our faith?
10. Can we ever escape from stress? Why?
11. Name someone you know who handles stress well.
12. Recall a time you successfully handled a stressful situation.
13. How does God want us to handle stress?

Practical Applications/Activities

1. List some strategies for overcoming stress.
2. Name ten causes of stress in your life. Rank them in order.
3. List the dangers of stress.
4. Develop a list of ways to help someone who is under stress.
5. Locate some verses in the Bible that are good to remember when under stress.

Prayer: *Dear God, thank you for putting stress in our lives and for giving us the ability to cope with it. May we know we can always turn to you for help in any situation. Be with us this week. Amen.*

Chapter 12

Can the World See Your Vision?

Chapter Summary

1. By living your faith the world can see your vision.
2. Where there is no morality, the people perish.
3. Where there is no hope, the people perish.
4. Where there is no love, the people perish.

Discussion Questions

1. What new insights did you receive from reading this chapter?
2. In your own words, explain what vision means to you.
3. What lessons do we learn from Proverbs 29:14-18?
4. What is so important about having vision?
5. Recall a time that you had vision and took action.
6. What are the benefits of having vision?
7. What are the costs of having vision?
8. Name someone you know who has vision.
9. How does God want us to use our vision?
10. What part can we as Christians play in returning a vision to our nation?
11. How did our nation and our people lose their vision? What was the cause?
12. Why are hope and love essential to our survival?

Practical Applications/Activities

1. Discuss what you see as signs of hope for our nation and world.
2. Decide to do one act this week toward positive change.

3. Carry a cross in your pocket this week to remind you of hope in Christ.
4. Help write a vision for your church or a group within your church.
5. Perform an act of volunteerism this week within your community.

Prayer: *Jesus, thank you for giving us a vision of a better world and the words and actions to bring about positive change. Help us to work together to bring the world closer to you. Amen.*

Chapter 13

Can the World See Your Servant Spirit?

Chapter Summary

1. By living your faith the world can see your servant spirit.
2. A Christian servant is committed to serving God.
3. A Christian servant is responsive to the needs of others.
4. A Christian servant is willing to pay the price.

Discussion Questions

1. What new insights did you receive from reading this chapter?
2. In your own words, explain what it is to have a servant spirit.
3. Tell about a person you know who demonstrates a servant spirit.
4. Discuss your reaction to Mark 1:16-20.
5. What part does sacrifice play in having a servant spirit?

6. How would you define Christian service?
7. Why does Christianity emphasize service to others?
8. What are the risks and costs of serving others?
9. List some famous Christian servants in the Bible and living today.
10. What are some roadblocks that deter people from serving others?
11. Recall an act of Christian service that someone performed for you.
12. How do we benefit from serving others?

Practical Applications/Activities

1. Donate one of your talents to your church this week.
2. Write a letter of commitment to being a servant to others.
3. List the needs of your community. Act on one of the needs.
4. Perform an act of service as a group or with your family.
5. Carry the letter "S" with you this week as a reminder of your service to others.

Prayer: *Dear God, thank you for our ability to serve others. Help us to be your servants in our church, at work, at home, and in our community. Show us how to give to others and work together with Christians in making this world better. Amen.*

Chapter 14

Can the World See Your Compassion?

Chapter Summary

1. By living your faith the world can see your compassion.
2. Compassion means being sensitive to the needs of others.

3. Compassion takes advantage of interruptions.
4. Compassion is being gracious.

Discussion Questions

1. What new insights did you receive from reading this chapter?
2. In your own words, explain what it means to have compassion.
3. Name someone who showed you compassion.
4. What lessons do we learn from Luke 8:40-48?
5. Recall a time that you showed compassion to someone. How did it feel?
6. Why did Jesus call loving compassion a sign of discipleship?
7. What are the risks and the costs of having compassion?
8. What does it mean to take advantage of interruptions?
9. Name some famous people who had compassion for others.
10. What does it mean to be gracious?
11. Recall a time that someone was gracious to you. How did you feel?
12. Discuss: Compassion is love at work.

Practical Applications/Activities

1. Discuss some ways you can be more sensitive to the needs of others.
2. Look up acts of compassion by Jesus in the Bible.
3. Take advantage of an interruption this week.
4. Thank someone who had compassion for you in the past.
5. Perform an act of compassion this week.

Prayer: *Dear God, thank you for your compassion toward us and your world. May we be compassionate toward others* *and use the actions of Jesus as our model. Help us to be more sensitive and take action to help those in need. Amen.*

Chapter 15

Can the World See Your Perseverance?

Chapter Summary

1. By living your faith the world can see your perseverance.
2. Persevere with goodness.
3. Persevere with graciousness.
4. Don't give up on God.

Discussion Questions

1. What new insights did you receive from reading this chapter?
2. What lessons and insights are found in Matthew 25:14-29?
3. Discuss the meaning of perseverance as a Christian.
4. Tell about a time you practiced perseverance. What were the results?
5. What are some of the common obstacles to perseverance?
6. Name some people in the Bible who persevered.
7. What are the costs of perseverance?
8. What are the benefits of perseverance?
9. What is so important about being gracious?
10. Why do you think the author selected this as his final topic?
11. Explain what graciousness and goodness mean to you. How are they different?
12. Recall a time when you were tempted to give up on God.

Practical Applications/Activities

1. Discuss what you learned by studying this book.
2. Perform an act of perseverance this week at home.
3. Read a book about someone who practiced perseverance.
4. Tell a child about the importance of perseverance.
5. Resolve to accomplish one objective that you have
   been postponing.

Prayer: *Jesus, we thank you for this group and our time
together. Thank you for the sharing, the love, and the search-
ing we did together. Be with us as we go our separate ways.
Help us to remember your love and desire for us to make a
difference in your world. Amen.*